Business Law

MARKET LEADER

Business English

A Robin Widdowson

Pearson Education Limited
Edinburgh Gate
Harlow
Essex CM20 2JE
England
and Associated Companies throughout the world.

www.pearsonlongman.com

First published 2010

ISBN 978-1-408-22005-4

Set in Metaplus, Times & ITC Cheltenham

Printed in Slovakia by Neografia

Acknowledgements

This series was developed and written by consultants working with LTS Training and Consulting, Bath, a specialist language and intercultural training company.

The author and publishers are grateful to Natalie Riddick who reported on earlier drafts of this material.

The author would like to thank Judy Bowles for the very welcome support and patience, Barbara Widdowson for encouragement, and Adrian Pilbeam for the opportunity to write this.

We are grateful to the following for permission to reproduce copyright material:

Text

Extract in Unit 2 adapted from 'Company lawyers get a wider role in business', *The Financial Times*, 14 July 2005 (Murray, S.), copyright © Sarah Murray; Extract in Unit 2 from 'Areas of activity for corporate lawyers', *The Financial Times*, 14 July 2005 (Murray, S.), copyright © Sarah Murray; Extract in Unit 3 (page 15) adapted from Doc No Ecom 12-00 'Alternative dispute resolution in the context of electronic commerce', February 2000, www.tacd.org, copyright © TACD; Extract in Unit 5 from 'Bollywood witnesses increases lawyer representation', *The Economic Times*, 13 October 2007 (Ganguly, D.), copyright © 2010, Bennett, Coleman & Co. Ltd. All rights reserved; Extract in Unit 12 from 'General duties of employers to their employees' under Health and Safety at Work Act 1974, Crown Copyright material is reproduced with permission under the terms of the Click-Use License; Extracts in Unit 13 from *Contract Law*, 5th edition, Longman (Elliott, C. and Quinn, F. 2005) copyright © Pearson Education Ltd; Extract in Unit 15 from *Business Law*, 2nd edition, Longman (Macintyre, E. 2004) copyright © Pearson Education Ltd; Extract in Unit 18 adapted from 'Leap of faith', *The Lawyer*, 27 October 2008 (Bi, F. and Atta, A.), www.thelawyer.com, copyright © The Lawyer.

The Financial Times

Extract in Unit 3 from 'Arbitration preferred in cross-border dispute', *The Financial Times*, 16 May 2006 (Tait, N.), copyright © The Financial Times Ltd; Extract in Unit 4 from 'Right and wrong choices in the market for justice', *The Financial Times*, 21 March 2006 (Kay, J.), copyright © The Financial Times Ltd; Extract in Unit 6 from 'Lawyer at GE seeks $500m in gender-bias case', *The Financial Times*, 31 May 2007 (Masters, B. and Guerrera, F.), copyright © The Financial Times Ltd; Extract in Unit 6 adapted from 'EU employment law advice', *The Financial Times*, 25 April 2008 (Moghadassi, R. and Robinson, W.), copyright © The Financial Times Ltd; Extract in Unit 7 from 'InBev ruling sparks fears for M&A in China', *The Financial Times*, 30 November 2008 (Tucker, S.), copyright © The Financial Times Ltd; Extract in Unit 9 from 'Diageo wins whisky piracy case in China', *The Financial Times*, 27 November 2008 (Anderlini, J.), copyright © The Financial Times Ltd; Extract in Unit 9 adapted from 'Rise in cases to protect companies' copyright', *The Financial Times*, 21 November 2008 (Moules, J.), copyright © The Financial Times Ltd; Extract in Unit 10 from 'Thinking about fraud', *The Financial Times*, 17 October 2008 (Peel, M.), copyright © The Financial Times Ltd; Extract in Unit 11 from 'Industry warns on EU pollution law', *The Financial Times*, 7 January 2008 (Bounds, A.), copyright © The Financial Times Ltd; Extract in Unit 16 adapted from 'Secrets of success', *The Financial Times*, 26 March 2009 (Burton, J.), copyright © The Financial Times Ltd; Extract in Unit 17 from 'Insider dealing sentence highlights crackdown', *The Financial Times*, 4 January 2008 (White, B.), copyright © The Financial Times Ltd.

In some instances we have been unable to trace the owners of copyright material, and we would appreciate any information that would enable us to do so.

Photos

The publisher would like to thank the following for their kind permission to reproduce their photographs:

(Key: b-bottom; c-centre; l-left; r-right; t-top)

Alamy Images: Ilian Food & Drink 37, moodboard 41; **Corbis**: Denis O'Regan 53; **DK Images**: Ian O'Leary 29; **iStockphoto**: 69, Anthony Baggett 17, Alexander Hafemann 9, Hazlan Abdul Hakim 45b, Lari Kemiläinen 33, Catherine Yeulet 73; **Jupiter Unlimited**: Stockxpert 13, 65, Thinkstock Images 45t; **PunchStock**: Digital Vision 25; **Rex Features**: Everett / c. Eros International 21; **shutterstock**: JustASC 5

Every effort has been made to trace the copyright holders and we apologise in advance for any unintentional omissions. We would be pleased to insert the appropriate acknowledgement in any subsequent edition of this publication.

Cover photo © Getty Images/Jeff Spielman

Project managed by Chris Hartley

Exercises marked with this symbol are designed to cover skills required for the ILEC reading test.

Contents

UNIT 1 Business and the law

Businesses cannot be run without taking into account the many laws and regulations, codes and standards that have been developed over the years to regulate the way commerce operates throughout the world. This unit looks at the way businesses are affected by legal issues.

BEFORE YOU READ

Discuss these questions.

1 In what ways will the law have an involvement in the different departments of an international manufacturing company? For example, the HR department will be concerned with contracts of employment. What about the Sales department? Or the Finance department? Come up with one or two ideas for each department.

2 What kinds of legal claim might be made against a company by employees, suppliers or competitors? And what claims might the company make against them?

READING

A Understanding the main points

Read the article on the opposite page and answer these questions.

1 Which four general areas of running a business are typically affected by the law?

2 How would you describe Elegance to someone who knew nothing about it, in about 10 words?

B Understanding details

Read the article again and answer these questions.

1 What kind of products does Elegance sell which have more than simple cosmetic properties? Why is this important?

2 Which people are described as being affected by the law (both inside and outside the company)?

3 What is important from a legal point of view about the way a job is advertised?

4 What kind of responsibilities does a manufacturing company have towards consumers?

5 What is important from a legal point of view about how products are advertised?

6 Why is intellectual property law important for companies like Elegance?

7 Which laws are relevant for Elegance as regards the working environment in its offices and factories?

8 What can companies do to reduce the amount of tax they have to pay?

How does the law affect the business world?

Introduction

A An interesting way to understand the wide-ranging effect that laws, regulations and codes have on the day-to-day operations of a business is to create a fictitious company, then consider how different aspects of that company come into contact with the law.

B Let's say our company is an international cosmetics organisation, Elegance, based in Paris, with offices in Europe, Asia, the Middle East and North America, and manufacturing plants in Europe, China, India and South America. The company makes and sells a wide range of creams, soaps, perfumes and hair treatments, all available under several famous brand names. It also produces medicated skin-care products; these are manufactured in Central Europe, and contain medicinal ingredients used under licence from a pharmaceutical company.

C To get a broad picture of how the law can have an impact on a company like Elegance, we can divide the organisation into four general areas: people, products, premises ... and profit.

People

D Here, we think about employees, management, shareholders and customers. Elegance has employees in its factories and offices, so they will require contracts of employment. Before anybody can be recruited for a job, the position is advertised – the HR department will be aware of strict laws relating to discrimination, diversity and equal opportunities. If an employee is guilty of misconduct, then employment law disciplinary procedures must be observed, followed sometimes by dismissal.

E The company is run by the directors and management; they are obliged to fulfil certain duties and to perform in a responsible way on behalf of the shareholders, the ultimate owners of the company. The directors must keep proper records of the financial status of the company; the company's legal status will govern what information is made available to the public.

F The people who buy and use Elegance products expect them to be safe and reliable. These customers have rights under consumer protection laws.

Products

G Poor quality control may result in a serious product liability claim against Elegance, perhaps involving a substantial award for damages. In addition to quality control, the company must consider advertising, packaging and labelling requirements. Elegance must closely monitor what it says about its products, and how it is said. Pharmaceutical products will need to comply with strict medicines legislation. Elegance factories will have contracts for the supply of raw materials; breach of contract may lead to litigation. The company must carefully protect its intellectual property rights – it wants to avoid infringement of patents, trademarks and copyright.

Premises

H Consider Elegance's premises – its land and buildings. Is Elegance owner of the real estate, or does it rent offices or factories? As an employer, Elegance must observe health and safety legislation in the factories and in the offices. It has a duty to provide employees with a safe working environment.

Profit

I A principal aim of an organisation such as Elegance is to make money every year. Corporation tax is payable on profits – tax lawyers can arrange schemes for legal tax avoidance, but not tax evasion. That is a criminal offence.

Conclusion

J This rapid tour round the fictional cosmetics company Elegance should demonstrate that very few aspects of running a typical commercial enterprise escape the influence of the law. It is essential for every company to keep itself fully informed of all relevant laws and regulations.

VOCABULARY

A Word search

Find words or phrases in the article which fit these meanings.

1 rules of conduct or correct business practice which don't have the force of law (paragraph A)
2 with permission of (another company) (paragraph B)
3 agreements between employers and employees (paragraph D)
4 employed, hired (paragraph D)
5 unfairly choosing one person in favour of another (paragraph D)
6 being fired (paragraph D)
7 the people who own a company (paragraph E)
8 the legal standing of a company (paragraph E)
9 a legal challenge resulting from a product that causes harm (paragraph G)
10 compensation ordered by a court to be paid to someone who has suffered loss or injury (paragraph G)
11 written laws (paragraph G)
12 when a contract is broken (paragraph G)
13 going to court (paragraph G)
14 copying someone's registered invention (paragraph G)
15 a word describing a building and the land it stands on (paragraph H)
16 property (offices, houses, etc.) (BrE) (paragraph H)
17 not to pay tax, but in an illegal manner (paragraph I)

B Word partnerships

Match the adjectives (1–5) with the nouns (a–e) to form word partnerships from the article.

1 equal	a) protection
2 disciplinary	b) estate
3 consumer	c) offence
4 real	d) procedure
5 criminal	e) opportunities

C Sentence completion

Use the word partnerships from Exercise B to complete these sentences.

1 The women in the office felt they hadn't been offered .... when compared with their male colleagues.
2 Saying your competitors make bad-quality products may be commercially unwise, but is it a ....?
3 We deal in offices, factories and other kinds of ....
4 He was late again! We will now have to follow the company .... and give him a written warning.
5 .... legislation has grown over the last 50 years. The buying public is now in a much stronger position.

D Legal terminology

1 **Complete the names of these different areas of law.**

1 the law relating to hiring and firing
e........ law
2 the law that protects the buying public
c........ law
3 the law regulating the manufacture and sale of pharmaceuticals
m........ law
4 the law relating to a share of profits paid to the state
t........ law
5 the law concerning the well-being of employees
h........ and s........ law

2 **Complete these legal expressions using the correct prepositions. Check your answers with the article.**

1 Their products are made .... licence.
2 One of our employees was guilty .... serious misconduct.
3 A member of the public made a claim .... the company.
4 All manufacturers must comply .... the new safety regulations.
5 The suppliers did not deliver the goods on the agreed date. It was a clear breach .... contract.

OVER TO YOU

1 Think of a well-known manufacturing company in your country. Give a five-minute presentation explaining the general areas of your country's law that the company needs to observe.
2 Discuss with a colleague what you think the legal differences are between managing a large manufacturing company, such as Elegance, and a small company, such as a consultancy, with about 10 staff, providing service only to local people from one office.

UNIT 2

In-house lawyers

This unit looks at how in-house corporate lawyers are nowadays called upon to use more than purely legal skills.

BEFORE YOU READ

Discuss these questions.

1. How do you become an in-house lawyer in your country? Why might a lawyer prefer to work in a company, rather than in a firm of lawyers?
2. What factors might influence a company in the decision to have its own in-house legal team?
3. Corporate social responsibility (CSR) concerns the way a company carries out its business – for example, it might be taking part in a social programme that benefits the community. What other 'socially responsible' activities do you think a company might involve itself in?

READING

A Understanding the main points

Read the article on the opposite page and answer these questions.

1. Why are company lawyers being asked to take a broader role in the companies they work for?
2. Who favours corporate lawyers taking a wider role, and who believes lawyers may not be the right people to make CSR decisions?
3. Which areas of business are represented in the article?

B Understanding details

Read the article again and answer these questions.

1. At the end of paragraph A, Ms Karp says, 'I haven't had to do that for several years.' What is she talking about?
2. Which two examples are given to illustrate how corporate liability is becoming more extensive?
3. Mr Rudolph says lawyers can be strategic-thought leaders. What is the result of their having this skill?
4. What were the findings of the research carried out by CMS Cameron McKenna?
5. What is the job of the in-house lawyer in relation to outside suppliers?
6. Which areas of risk management are some in-house lawyers becoming involved in?
7. What is Bill Carr's argument against in-house lawyers being involved in CSR issues?
8. What is Elliot Schrage's argument in favour of lawyers' involvement in such issues?
9. What action does Jeffrey Kindler think companies must take in respect of developing social issues, and why?

Company lawyers get a wider role in business

by Sarah Murray

A As an in-house legal adviser, Roberta Schuhalter Karp used to feel she had to justify her presence at corporate social responsibility meetings to her colleagues. 'I would say: "I'm not wearing my legal hat now – I just have a broader role within the company",' says the Vice-President of Corporate Affairs and general counsel at Liz Claiborne, the clothing company. 'I haven't had to do that for several years.'

B Ms Karp is not alone in having broadened her role. As corporate liability expands to include issues from breaches of labour practice codes in developing countries to health concerns over weight problems in the West, senior lawyers are regular participants in meetings to discuss them.

C 'Companies have their in-house lawyers with them at the table as part of the team,' says Phillip Rudolph, partner in the corporate social responsibility practice at Foley Hoag, a Washington DC-based law firm. 'Because, depending on the role the lawyer plays and the value they are perceived to add to the management team, they can be strategic-thought leaders.'

D In a recent survey conducted by CMS Cameron McKenna, a UK-based law firm, one-third of senior executives said that while the Chief Executive has overall responsibility for corporate social responsibility, in-house lawyers come second. More than half the respondents said in-house lawyers should take a lead on corporate responsibility.

E In-house lawyers are also busy drafting company codes of conduct, ensuring compliance with regulations and producing documentation to ensure the standards of third-party suppliers meet those of their clients. As well as working on compliance and contract diligence, in-house lawyers are also helping companies take a broader approach to managing social and environmental risks.

F The problem is that these risks are complex and without easy answers, as the experiences of companies in the clothing industry illustrate. Companies such as Liz Claiborne, Gap and Nike are among those that have been targeted by anti-sweatshop campaigners.

G 'Corporate lawyers may not have all the skill sets required to assess social and environmental issues affecting companies, which is why CSR should be considered by a wider group of personnel,' says Bill Carr, partner at CMS Cameron McKenna.

H At the same time, because of their training and experience, lawyers can bring a more objective perspective to ethical issues than others in the management team.

I A lawyer and business strategist who was formerly Senior Vice-President of Global Affairs at Gap, Elliot Schrage, argues that there is another good reason for getting legal departments involved. He says that legal training leads to rigorous thinking and analysis, which have so far not been a strong point in corporate responsibility and sustainability initiatives.

J Jeffrey Kindler, Vice-Chairman and general counsel at Pfizer, the pharmaceuticals company, believes that the requirements of the law and the demands of society for change in corporate behaviour are no longer separate matters for concern. 'We have to understand, anticipate and respond to these emerging social issues before they become legal issues or crises.'

FT

VOCABULARY

A Word search

Find words or phrases in the article which fit these meanings.

1 'I'm not here in my capacity as a lawyer' (paragraph A)
2 an American expression meaning 'senior legal adviser' (paragraph A)
3 the legal responsibilities of a company (paragraph B)
4 matters, problems (paragraph B)
5 rules of conduct, without the force of law (paragraph B)
6 a law firm, or a specialised part of a law firm (paragraph C)
7 total, covering everything as a whole (paragraph D)
8 writing (usually a preliminary version) (paragraph E)
9 describes people or organisations from outside (paragraph E)
10 checking that contracts meet requirements (paragraph E)
11 a workplace where workers are exploited, working long hours in poor conditions for low pay (paragraph F)
12 a senior member of a law firm (paragraph G)
13 not influenced by personal wishes or feelings (paragraph H)
14 relating to moral, rather than commercial, values (paragraph H)

B Word families

Complete the chart with words from the article.

noun	verb
........[1]	to breach
........[2]	to comply
assessment	........[3]
anticipation	........[4]
response	........[5]

C Sentence completion

Use words from Exercise B in the correct form to complete these sentences.

1 It is essential to check that we have fully .... with the new regulations.
2 The .... to our survey was better than expected. Over 60% of people contacted gave their opinions.
3 If they do not deliver on time, they will be in .... of their agreement with us.
4 It's sometimes difficult to .... how effective a new law is.
5 Don't think only about what we as suppliers want. You must also .... what they as purchasers might be looking for. That way, we might come to an acceptable agreement.

ILEC

D Text completion

Choose the best word to fill the gap from the choices A–D below the extract.

Areas of activity for corporate lawyers

Litigation: ....[1] based on alleged failures to comply with ethical standards.
Codes of conduct: ensuring company compliance with both legal ....[2] and in-house obligations to behave ethically in all business activities.
Contract governance: incorporation of a company's codes of conduct and ethical practices into contracts with third-party suppliers to ....[3] they follow the same ethical standards.
Risk management: identification of potential liabilities that might affect a company's reputation, share price and licence to operate, and ....[4] of advice on how to mitigate such risks.
Board awareness: potential for senior corporate lawyers to bring broader issues of sustainability and corporate responsibility to the attention of the Chief Executive and ....[5] of the board.

FT

	A	B	C	D
1	processes	judges	lawsuits	courts
2	laws	rules	demands	requirements
3	ensure	check	assure	request
4	supply	provision	managing	asking
5	participants	managers	directors	members

E Vocabulary development

Choose the best explanation for each word from the extract in Exercise D.

1 litigation (line 1)
a) taking legal action in court
b) written laws

2 alleged (line 2)
a) proved in court
b) claimed but not yet proved in court

3 obligations (line 7)
a) things you must not do
b) things you must do

4 governance (line 9)
a) controlling and guiding
b) preparing and writing

5 to mitigate (lines 21–22)
a) to eliminate
b) to reduce

6 sustainability (lines 25–26)
a) preservation of resources for future generations
b) maintaining high levels of profitability

OVER TO YOU

1 Explain to a colleague whether, in your country, it is easy to change from being an in-house lawyer to being a private or state lawyer, and vice versa. Which job would you prefer, and why?

2 Find out the main differences between a solicitor and a barrister in the English legal system, then compare their functions with an American attorney. Can they all become in-house lawyers? Present a brief overview to inform someone who is not a legal specialist.

3 Do some research so you can either give a brief presentation (five minutes) or write a short report (300 words) illustrating how a company can demonstrate that it is 'socially responsible'. Use real examples.

UNIT 3 Handling international disputes

This unit considers different ways of settling cross-border disputes between multinational companies. Instead of going to court, the companies can choose the arbitration process – a specially appointed person or panel decides how the matter should be resolved.

BEFORE YOU READ

Discuss these questions.

1. *A cross-border dispute* means a serious commercial disagreement between organisations based in different countries. What kind of disputes do you think are likely to affect multinationals?
2. What are the disadvantages of litigation between companies from different countries? Are there any advantages?
3. Why is arbitration sometimes thought to be better than going to court?

READING

A Understanding the main points

Read the article on the opposite page and answer these questions.

1. Where does all the information about corporate lawyers' preferences come from?
2. Is cost a main factor in preferring the arbitration process to litigation?
3. Do the majority of lawyers questioned prefer international arbitration or international litigation?

B Understanding details

Read the article again and answer these questions.

1. Name three key reasons for in-house general counsel to favour arbitration.
2. In which specific area are arbitration costs said to be at least the same as those for litigation?
3. How do lawyers feel about the idea of being able to appeal against arbitration decisions?
4. How does the article describe the general business environment at the time the report appears?
5. Are arbitration procedures becoming more common or less common? Provide some evidence to back up your answer.
6. Give details of the companies represented in the study.
7. Give details of the findings of the study.
8. What three reasons do lawyers give for avoiding litigation?
9. Are arbitration decisions always accepted without question?
10. Which reason was given as a cause for concern for both arbitration and litigation procedures?

Arbitration preferred in cross-border disputes

by Nikki Tait

A Three out of four top lawyers at multinational companies would prefer to settle cross-border commercial disputes by arbitration rather than litigation, because of the unpredictability of decisions made by local courts. Key reasons put forward in favour of international arbitration include: more flexible procedures; the lack of publicity surrounding hearings; and the better chances of enforcing any awards made by an arbitration panel.

B But many in-house general counsel say international arbitration is at least as expensive as litigation, particularly for fairly small disputes. Most also reject the idea of introducing an appeal system for arbitration decisions – appeals could help to remove some of the legal inconsistencies that exist between individual judgments, but they would inevitably add time and cost to the process.

C The findings are the result of a study commissioned by consultants PricewaterhouseCoopers (PwC), with research done by Queen Mary's School of International Arbitration at the University of London. The report comes as more companies invest abroad, and the complexity of cross-border disputes multiplies. As a result, there has been visible growth in the use of arbitration and other ADR (alternative dispute resolution) procedures – for example, the International Chamber of Commerce's dispute resolution service has seen more than 500 requests for arbitration annually in recent years. Many big law firms have also been increasing their capacity in this area.

D The study itself centres on the responses of more than 100 in-house general counsel at multinational corporations. About half of these were in Europe, 30 per cent in Asia, and 15 per cent in the Americas. Most had annual sales of at least $500m.

E According to the findings, 73 per cent of those questioned preferred to use international arbitration, either on its own or in conjunction with other dispute resolution mechanisms, such as mediation. By contrast, cross-border litigation was favoured by only 11 per cent. Gerry Lagerberg, PwC partner, said that this smaller group that still preferred litigation generally used very specialised courts – for example, patent courts – or operated mainly in countries with well-regarded court systems.

F The most commonly cited reason for the remainder to avoid litigation was 'anxiety about litigating under a foreign law before a court far from home' – although the cost and time involved and concern about lack of confidentiality were also mentioned.

G However, half the respondents also said cost was their main concern about arbitration. Surprisingly, two-thirds of the in-house lawyers believed this was more expensive than cross-border litigation, and another 23 per cent thought costs at least comparable.

H In spite of growing challenges to arbitration awards, 91 per cent of respondents rejected the idea of including an appeal mechanism in international arbitration, saying obtaining a final decision was more important.

VOCABULARY

A Understanding expressions

Choose the best explanation for each of these words and phrases from the text.

1 '... to *settle* cross-border commercial disputes ...' (lines 2–3)
   a) argue your position in a dispute
   b) agree a solution to the dispute

2 '... the lack of publicity surrounding *hearings* ...' (lines 9–10)
   a) court cases
   b) judges' decisions

3 '... between individual *judgments* ...' (line 21)
   a) court cases
   b) judges' decisions

4 ' ... other ADR (*alternative dispute resolution*) procedures ...' (lines 34–35)
   a) different kinds of dispute can be heard in a law court
   b) disputes are settled by an independent person or body, instead of in a law court

5 '... for example, *patent courts* ...' (lines 59–60)
   a) courts dealing with rights relating to inventions
   b) courts dealing with rights relating to trademarks

6 '... mainly in countries with *well-regarded court systems*.' (lines 60–61)
   a) famous court systems
   b) court systems which are thought to be good

7 'The *most commonly cited* reason for ...' (lines 62–63)
   a) criticised most frequently
   b) mentioned most often

8 '... *litigating* under a foreign law ...' (lines 64–65)
   a) bringing or defending a lawsuit
   b) enforcing legal regulations

9 '... rejected the idea of including *an appeal mechanism* ...' (lines 78–79)
   a) an automatic appeal system
   b) a system allowing appeals

10 '... obtaining *a final decision* ...' (lines 80–81)
   a) an official decision that can be appealed against
   b) an official decision with no appeal allowed

B Word partnerships

Match the verbs (1–5) with the nouns (a–e) to form common word partnerships often found in business law. Some verbs can be matched to more than one noun.

1 to settle	a) costs
2 to enforce	b) a case
3 to reject	c) a dispute
4 to add	d) a law
5 to cite	e) an argument

C Sentence completion

Use the word partnerships from Exercise B to complete these sentences.

1 It is often advisable to .... instead of taking another company to court.
2 The lawyer advised that obtaining a technical report was unnecessary, and would simply ....
3 The judge .... the .... put forward by the defence counsel, saying there was no clear evidence.
4 In court, counsel .... supporting his view that the transaction was not fraudulent.
5 That new speeding .... will not be effective if it is not ....!

ILEC D Word families

Use the words below the text to form one word that fits in each numbered gap.

Alternative dispute resolution in the context of electronic commerce

E-commerce makes it possible for consumers to *transact*[1] with companies or other individuals without regard to geographic location, but it also raises the question of how disputes will be ....[2], especially when the buyer and seller are physically distant. While the buying public are generally ....[3] by the laws of their jurisdictions, and commercial sellers are also subject to legal ....[4] in the countries in which they are located, cost and other factors may make it difficult for ....[5] to obtain a satisfactory solution in cross-border disputes. Alternative dispute resolution (ADR) can be very helpful to both parties in electronic transactions, especially in cross-border complaints. At the same time, consumers and those who ....[6] their interests must ....[7] the right to use the courts of the consumers' countries if necessary.

1 transaction
2 resolution
3 protective
4 oversee
5 consumption
6 representative
7 retention

E Prepositions

Complete these sentences using the correct prepositions, then check your answers in the text in Exercise D.

1 It is possible .... consumers to do business more easily. (lines 1–2)
2 Companies can transact .... other companies. (lines 2–3)
3 Individuals are protected .... the laws of their own countries. (line 11)
4 Sales of goods are made subject .... many legal requirements. (line 14)
5 ADR can be helpful .... all parties involved. (line 21)
6 He still has the right .... take another person to court. (line 27)

OVER TO YOU

1 Take notes of the key findings from the article, so you can give a short presentation about the PwC study.
2 Do some research to find out about different kinds of ADR, then write a report (about 300 words) summarising the topic.

UNIT 4 Different countries, different legal systems

This unit looks at how businesses, and individuals, can think about which country's legal system might regulate their activities, or which country might be best for a court hearing.

The legal power or authority of a country is known as its *jurisdiction*.

BEFORE YOU READ

Discuss these questions.

1 When companies enter into international commercial agreements, why is it important to decide on the applicable legal jurisdiction before contracts are signed?

2 When there is a dispute, court cases can sometimes be heard in a country where none of the parties lives or does business. Why should anyone choose to start an action in a country other than their own?

3 Why might developing countries and newly emerging economies want to ensure that their laws and regulations are 'business-friendly' towards foreign companies?

READING

A Understanding the main points

Read the article on the opposite page and answer these questions.

1 Why are legal systems in different countries said to be in competition with each other?

2 What exactly is meant by *choice of laws*? And how does that differ from *forum shopping*?

B Understanding details

Read the article again and answer these questions.

1 The Royal Courts of Justice are in London. Why did the three people mentioned in paragraph A use English law courts?

2 Does the writer feel that competition between legal systems of different countries is a normal business concept?

3 For what kind of business is English law commonly used?

4 How do English courts differ from courts in America in the way they interpret contracts?

5 Why have law firms in the City of London been able to market their services internationally?

6 Why does so much asbestos litigation take place in Jefferson County, Mississippi, USA, and how does this benefit the local community?

7 Does the European Union regard forum shopping in a positive way?

Right and wrong choices in the market for justice

Royal Courts of Justice, London

by John Kay

A Why is the American author Dan Brown in London to defend claims that he has breached the copyright of a New Zealander and a fellow American? Why did Frau Flick, former wife of a German industrialist, ask an English court to determine the terms of her divorce settlement? Why did Roman Polanski, a French citizen, come to the Royal Courts of Justice to seek libel damages from *Vanity Fair*, an American magazine? Each of them thought they would get a better deal in England than at home.

B In a global marketplace, the legal systems of different countries are in competition with each other. The notion of competition in the supply of justice is strange. Yet justice is an elusive concept, and there are many routes to it, all imperfect. Competition in legal services begins when, before they enter into a legal relationship, people and businesses search for the most appropriate legal framework. One element of that framework is the jurisdiction in which any dispute is to be resolved. This is the issue of the choice of laws.

C English law is very widely used in financial services, even for transactions that have no other connection with England. English law gives much more freedom to write whatever contract the parties want than the civil law systems of many other countries. English judges are strict in enforcing the terms of a contract, while courts in America pay more attention to the context of the transaction – the intentions of the parties and the reasonableness of the contract terms.

D This English combination of flexibility before the event and rigidity after it is attractive to many. English judges have also acquired a reputation for giving foreigners a fair chance in court. These competitive attractions of the English legal system have made City law firms large exporters of legal services.

E Competition through choice of laws is almost wholly desirable. The freedom of contract it allows has economic benefits, and competition encourages other countries to make their legal systems business friendly. Emerging states in Eastern Europe have used English law and modelled aspects of their post-communist codes on English principles.

F Choice of laws is made before a dispute arises. Forum shopping is when competition takes place after the dispute has occurred. If choice of laws has many benefits, forum shopping has many disadvantages. Jefferson County, Mississippi, is the world centre of asbestos litigation. Not because that community has been specially damaged by the effects of asbestos, but because its judges and juries are famously sympathetic to plaintiffs. They are encouraged to remain sympathetic by the economic benefits this depressed area derives from supplying motel rooms and pizzas to visiting attorneys.

G A jurisdiction benefits from forum shopping if its decisions are out of line with mainstream opinion, and the most common reason is that there is something wrong with its legal system. The 1980 Rome Convention, which governs contracts within the European Union, strikes a well-crafted balance: it encourages choice of laws, but discourages forum shopping. These principles are under attack from Europe's enthusiasts for harmonisation, from vested legal interests which resent the loss of business overseas and from politicians who would like to interfere in every dispute. In the market for justice, as for every other commodity, it is important to understand both the genius, and the limits, of competitive markets.

FT

VOCABULARY

A Understanding expressions

Choose the best explanation for each phrase from the article.

1 '... to *defend claims* that ...' (line 2)
   a) argue your position in a legal dispute against you
   b) start a court case against someone

2 '... has *breached the copyright* of ...' (line 3)
   a) used copyrighted material with permission
   b) used copyrighted material without permission

3 '... to *determine the terms* of ...' (line 7)
   a) bring those terms to an end
   b) decide exactly what the terms are

4 '... her *divorce settlement*?' (lines 7–8)
   a) agreement to get divorced
   b) arrangement setting out how money and property should be divided after divorce

5 'Yet justice is *an elusive concept* ...' (lines 19–20)
   a) an idea that is hard to define
   b) all about being fair

6 'One element of that framework is *the jurisdiction in which any dispute is to be resolved*.' (lines 25–28)
   a) the country whose law will apply if there is a dispute
   b) the way in which a dispute should be settled legally

7 '... much *more freedom to write whatever contract the parties want* than ...' (lines 33–35)
   a) fewer restrictions on who can enter into a contract
   b) fewer restrictions on what can be included in a contract

8 '... from *vested legal interests* which resent ...' (line 90)
   a) people or organisations that enjoy a benefit from the existing situation
   b) traditional lawyers who dislike change

B Legal terminology

Match these legal words and phrases (1–8) with their meanings (a–h).

1 copyright	a) legal structure
2 libel damages	b) opposite of *defendant* (also known as *claimant*)
3 to enter into a legal relationship	c) bringing lawsuits
4 legal framework	d) legal ownership of rights in literary, artistic and musical works
5 to enforce the terms of a contract	e) to begin a legal relationship
6 City law firms	f) to make sure the contractual terms are obeyed
7 litigation	g) compensation for an untrue published statement that harms someone's reputation
8 plaintiff	h) in England, large law firms based in London

C Sentence completion

Use the words and phrases from Exercise B in the correct form to complete these sentences.

1 She works in the .... department, so she spends a lot of time preparing documents and appearing in court.

2 Before a country joins the European Union, it has to consider whether its existing .... matches the requirements of the EU.

3 Some rock stars have been awarded substantial .... after newspapers have published untrue stories about them.

4 The majority of high-level international business deals in the UK are handled by .... rather than smaller firms located outside London.

5 The .... claimed in court that he had lost a considerable sum of money after being sold defective machinery by the defendant.

6 A recognised way of protecting .... is by using the © symbol, followed by the year the work is produced and the name of the person producing the work.

7 You need to be fully informed about the financial circumstances of a company before you .... with them.

8 The new supplying company repeatedly failed to meet their delivery obligations, so we had to go to court to ....

D Word families

Complete the chart with words from the article.

verb	noun
........[1]	defence
........[2]	determination
to settle	........[3]
........[4]	resolution
to transact	........[5]
........[6]	enforcement
to litigate	........[7]
........[8]	government

OVER TO YOU

1 The article tells us that when resolving disputes, different courts will not necessarily view the law in the same way. But what about completely different legal systems? The common law system (used in the USA and England, for example) is based on decisions made by the courts, whereas civil law (used in Latin America and continental Europe) is based on a written civil code. Discuss some of the key differences between these two systems.

2 The United States courts are famous for awarding enormous sums of money in cases where someone has been harmed by a manufacturer's faulty product, or when instructions for equipment do not include every warning imaginable. Consider the pros and cons of a legal system that allows such high levels of compensation to be awarded. If possible, provide examples of cases where substantial damages have been given by the court.

UNIT 5 Bollywood needs lawyers!

Bollywood is the Indian film industry's version of Hollywood, USA. This unit looks at how those involved in this often risky business are increasingly looking to lawyers to provide professional help.

BEFORE YOU READ

Discuss these questions.

1 The article talks about the film industry. What other areas of business and commerce are covered by entertainment lawyers?

2 Think of a recent highly successful movie. How can money be made from the film, in addition to showing it in its home market?

READING

A Understanding the main points

Read the article on the opposite page and answer these questions.

1 Why do members of the film industry in India's Bollywood increasingly need advice from lawyers?

2 In what ways does the Bollywood film industry differ from Hollywood, as far as lawyers' services are concerned?

B Understanding details

Read the article again and answer these questions.

1 Why did people in the Indian film industry not want to consult lawyers for business advice?

2 What does Ashni Parekh see as a key factor in running a successful law practice for the Indian film industry?

3 What first caused the change away from a simple one-page contract or a handshake to seal a deal?

4 What did the courts show was the problem with many of those early, simple contracts?

5 What business developments have resulted in the film industry becoming a far more complicated environment?

6 What are some clients being advised to do to create a tax advantage?

7 What are the problems a typical Hollywood contract would present in India?

8 The article mentions various areas of work that Indian entertainment lawyers can be involved in. What are they?

Bollywood witnesses increased lawyer representation

by Dibeyendu Ganguly

A Two years ago, when Ashni Parekh left Nishith Desai and Associates, its entertainment law practice wasn't exactly flourishing. A newly corporatised Bollywood wanted legal advice, but was still not used to paying high legal fees. 'It was obvious that charging Indian film makers $200 an hour was not going to work,' says Parekh, who has since launched out on her own. 'You have to adapt your practice to suit this industry, which is extremely personality driven.'

B Parekh now operates from home, and business is booming. She says, 'I get a new client every day, including people who are new to the industry and signing a contract for the first time.'

C There was a time when a legal contract in Bollywood was a simple affair. The producer signed a standard one-page deal with the record company for the music rights and another deal with the distributor for distribution to the cinema screens.

D More important than the paper was the handshake, for nobody was really interested in taking anyone to court. The cosy arrangement collapsed with the coming of home-viewing technology; this then led to litigation to determine whether the rights to video were vested with the producer or the distributor. The courts said it depended on the contracts, and for the most part, the contracts loosely gave away 'all rights' to distributors and record companies, with no provision for new technologies.

E Today, things are getting more complicated, with revenues from ring tones exceeding the revenue from music sales, foreign distribution – including screening on aeroplanes and cruise liners – becoming more profitable than domestic distribution, and actors earning as much from product endorsements as films. 'Bollywood is definitely signing more contracts than before, though we are still a long way from the Hollywood model, where everyone is represented by a lawyer,' says Anand Desai of DSK Legal.

F DSK is also advising its film-industry clients on tax. For example, with Indian films gaining increasing revenues from abroad, some producers are looking at the option of vesting the rights to their films in a Mauritius-based company, thereby putting their films on the same level as Hollywood films for tax purposes.

G Whenever you hear of an aggrieved party taking a producer to court or stalling the release of a film, you can bet Ameet Naik is somehow involved. Formerly a lawyer with DSK, Naik is doing highly specialised work in numerous areas of entertainment law. One of his new clients is Endemol, the UK-based producer of entertainment formats for the worldwide market.

H Needless to say, entertainment lawyers are relying heavily on well-established international precedents as they move into new areas. Hollywood contracts are long and complicated, so much of the lawyer's time and effort goes into figuring out what stays and what goes out. 'You can't just cut and paste Hollywood clauses into Indian contracts,' says Naik. 'Hollywood contracts have far too many words. You need to reduce the amount of legalese and make it comprehensible to the client. A 50-page contract just wouldn't work in India.'

from *The Economic Times*

VOCABULARY

A Word search

Find words or phrases in the article which fit these meanings.

1 a law office that specialises in advising people working in films, musicals, TV shows, etc. (paragraph A)
2 large amounts of money payable for legal services (paragraph A)
3 a normal one-page agreement (paragraph C)
4 starting legal proceedings against (paragraph D)
5 court action (paragraph D)
6 to decide (paragraph D)
7 owned by (paragraph D)
8 without providing for (paragraph D)
9 considering the possibility of transferring the legal ownership of (paragraph F)
10 someone who feels they have a reason to complain (paragraph G)
11 specialist legal terminology (paragraph H)
12 understandable (paragraph H)

B Understanding expressions

Choose the best explanation for each word or phrase from the article.

1 '... wasn't exactly *flourishing*.' (lines 3–4)
   a) growing
   b) failing
2 '... the music *rights* ...' (line 23)
   a) manufacturing and production systems
   b) the legal entitlement to sell or trade something (a commercial asset)
3 '... earning as much from *product endorsements* ...' (lines 47–48)
   a) allowing your name to be used to sell products
   b) doing extra work, such as opening new stores, appearing at public functions, etc.
4 '... or *stalling* the release of a film ...' (lines 64–65)
   a) cancelling
   b) deliberately delaying
5 '... well-established international *precedents* ...' (lines 74–75)
   a) examples, e.g. of contracts, that have already been established
   b) leading legal experts
6 'You can't just *cut and paste* ...' (lines 80–81)
   a) copy blocks of text
   b) change original wording
7 '... Hollywood *clauses* ...' (line 81)
   a) rules and regulations
   b) paragraphs in a contract

C Sentence completion

Use the words and phrases from Exercise B in the correct form to complete these sentences.

1 He said his work was about art, not money, but now that actor has done a .... His name is on some kind of washing powder!
2 Look at the contract and check the .... on insurance risks. We must know exactly what the terms are.
3 Their new computer consultancy business is really .... It has been a success from the word go.
4 This wording looks completely wrong for a contract. I think they have just .... text from a sales brochure!
5 Do we already have a .... for an agreement like this? If so, we needn't write a completely new document.
6 The sellers say they can't find our order, but I think they're just .... They want more time to find a solution.
7 You could make a lot of money selling the distribution .... to that movie in China!

D Legal terminology

Use words from the article to complete these sentences.

1 A client consults a lawyer, and the lawyer gives .... to the client.
2 After advising a client, a lawyer charges a ....
3 In the world of entertainment, we talk about not only signing a contract, but also signing a ....
4 A contract contains many ...., which are similar to paragraphs.
5 When writing a new contract, we look to see if there are already good examples of clauses from existing contracts that we can use; these examples are called ....
6 Legal language which some clients cannot easily understand is informally known as ....
7 In court, a client is .... by a lawyer. The lawyer acts on the client's behalf.
8 The field of law involving court cases is known as ....

OVER TO YOU

1 A film actor is a person who works in the world of art, culture and creativity, but who can definitely benefit from a good head for business. What other occupations might also need sound business and legal advice, and what can happen if it is not available?
2 You are business adviser to a young, enthusiastic, intelligent pop singer who has just won the first round of a TV talent competition. You have five minutes to present to her the key business areas she should be thinking about if she goes on to be a great success.

UNIT 6

Practising diversity

This unit looks at 'practising diversity', which means, in effect, an employer giving equal opportunities to employees from different kinds of minority group.

BEFORE YOU READ

Discuss these questions.

1 What examples of minority groups do you know?

2 What are the benefits to society of making sure that minority groups are not discriminated against when companies hire new staff?

3 Do you think the law is the best way of ensuring there is no discrimination in society? What other ways are there, and how effective are they?

READING

A Understanding the main points

1 **Read the article on the opposite page and answer these questions.**

   1 Why exactly did Lorene Schaefer feel she had been discriminated against? Give details.

   2 How would you describe Ms Schaefer's career profile? Are there others like her in the American business world?

2 **Which of the following 'challenges' faced by businesswomen are mentioned in the article?**

   1 working in a male-dominated world

   2 not being employed by major corporations

   3 not being paid the same as male counterparts

   4 being offered only junior positions

   5 experiencing difficulty in reaching the most senior positions

B Understanding details

Read the article again and say whether these statements are true (T) or false (F). Correct the false ones.

1 The lawyer claiming compensation has a high position in her company.

2 The claim also asks for compensation for other lawyers at the company.

3 She was told she did not have the right academic qualifications for the job in question.

4 Women form a large part of senior management at GE.

5 Until filing this suit, Ms Schaefer believed she had been on her way to a top position.

6 GE feels it must accept what she says.

7 GE has received an award for promoting female employees.

8 Class actions (cases brought on behalf of a group of people) are well suited to this sort of discrimination claim.

Lawyer at GE seeks $500m in gender-bias case

by Brooke Masters
and Francesco Guerrera

A One of the highest-ranking female lawyers at General Electric filed a sex-discrimination lawsuit against the company on Thursday, seeking $500m in damages on behalf of herself and 1,500 upper-level female executives and attorneys at the company.

B Lorene Schaefer filed her lawsuit, which seeks to be certified as a class action, after learning in April that she would be demoted from her position as General Counsel of GE's transportation division. She said she was told she was not 'big enough' for her job.

C The lawsuit could prove embarrassing to GE, which has been doing its best to lose its old image of a male-dominated industrial conglomerate.

D Ms Schaefer's complaint, filed by the lawyers Sanford Wittels and Heisler, alleges the two female divisional general counsels were paid less and kept at a lower rank than five male counterparts. They also contend that women are underrepresented in GE's top ranks, making up 13 per cent of senior corporate officers and 20 per cent of senior band executives, the next level down. 'The General Electric company does not meet and deliver the results in diversity for women,' Ms Schaefer said.

E She had worked at the company for 13 years and 'believed that I was one of the women moving through the glass ceiling,' until she was informed she was going to be replaced by a 'big-time GC [general counsel]'.

F GE said it 'strongly' denied the allegations and would defend itself against the claims in court. 'Ms Schaefer's career with GE clearly illustrates the opportunities that the company provides to women, as she was given opportunities to move to progressively larger roles,' a GE spokesman said. 'GE works very hard to promote and ensure diversity in our company. There are more women in bigger jobs at GE than ever before.' In 2004, GE was given an award by Catalyst, an organisation dedicated to promoting women in business, for its efforts in increasing the number of female corporate officers.

G Ms Schaefer is one of a growing number of women who have done well in corporate America and then filed complaints after encountering difficulty reaching the highest levels, said Joe Sellars, an employment attorney who represents plaintiffs.

H Such high-level cases can be harder to bring as class actions because promotion decisions are of a more individual nature, lawyers said.

FT

C Finding figures

What do these figures and dates refer to in the article?

a) $500m
b) 1,500
c) 13%
d) 20%
e) 13
f) 2004

VOCABULARY

A Legal terminology

Find words or phrases in the article which fit these meanings.

1 started a court case (paragraph A)
2 trying to obtain compensation (of a certain amount of money) (paragraph A)
3 a legal action brought on behalf of a group of people (paragraph B)
4 a senior in-company legal adviser (AmE) (paragraph B)
5 claims something in a legal process, before it is proved (paragraph D)
6 argue or maintain that a certain situation applies (paragraph D)
7 offering equal opportunities to minority groups (in employment) (paragraph D)
8 the invisible barrier that stops certain groups of people (mainly women) from being promoted (paragraph E)
9 appear in court to state its case, following a claim against it (paragraph F)
10 a US lawyer working in the area of 'hiring and firing' (paragraph G)
11 acts on behalf of someone, for example in a court case (paragraph G)
12 people who make a legal complaint in court (paragraph G)

B Word families

Complete the chart.

verb	noun
........[1]	(law)suit
........[2]	complaint
........[3]	allegation
........[4]	contention
........[5]	denial
........[6]	defence
........[7]	representation

C Sentence completion

Use words from Exercise B in the correct form to complete these sentences.

1 They made several .... of unlawful practice.
2 The company .... that they discriminated against female employees.
3 This is a serious claim against your company. You will need proper legal ...., a skilled lawyer.
4 Her lawyers filed a formal ....
5 One .... was that male employees were paid more.
6 Last year, she .... the company for discrimination.
7 They hired the best lawyers to .... them in court against the claims.

ILEC **D**

Text completion

Choose the best word to fill the gap from the choices A–D below the extract.

EU employment law advice

Ramyar Moghadassi and Wendy Robinson, partners at Peregrine Law LLP, London

Employment discrimination laws are not unique to the UK. In fact, in large part due to European Union (EU) ....[1], all member states of 5 the EU have some sort of employment discrimination ....[2] in place, covering areas such as race, sex, disability, age, religious beliefs and sexual orientation. Non-EU countries, such as Switzerland and Nor- 10 way, also have similar employment laws. The main difference between the employment discrimination laws in these countries is the way in which 15 they are enforced and the ....[3] awarded in successful claims.

In the UK, there is no upper limit to the awards allowable to a successful ....[4] in an employment 20 discrimination case. Generally, other EU countries tend to be less litigious. Also, by contrast, damages in European employment discrimination ....[5] are generally far lower.

25 A responsible employer should seek the ....[6] of specialist lawyers. This is especially important, given new entrants into the EU. For example, Poland does not have laws 30 prohibiting discrimination on the basis of sexual orientation in the same way as other EU countries.

	A	B	C	D
1	statutes	orders	declarations	directives
2	texts	legislation	regulation	codes
3	fine	damage	damages	sentences
4	litigant	lawyer	prosecutor	complainer
5	defences	claimants	claims	rules
6	consultancy	fee	advise	advice

E

Vocabulary development

1 **Look again at the article about the female lawyer on page 25. Find words meaning the following.**

   1 the opposite of *promoted*
   2 the opposite of *admitted*

2 **What is a synonym for the word *bias* in the title, which can also be used in cases of discrimination?**

3 **Look again at the article about EU employment law above. Find two words formed from the word *litigate* and explain what they mean.**

4 **Without looking at the above article again, list as many different categories of employment discrimination as you can recall (six are mentioned). Then check your answers against the article.**

OVER TO YOU

1 If you were advising a company about employment discrimination, what practical tips would you give it for its recruitment procedure? Write out a list. Think about the wording of job offers, and the interview process.

2 Sometimes companies can 'over-compensate' and go out of their way to employ people from minority groups. This is known as positive discrimination. What could be the possible consequences of favouring certain groups of people in this way?

UNIT 7

International mergers and acquisitions

This unit looks at how an international acquisition is affected by antitrust rules in China.

BEFORE YOU READ

Discuss these questions.

1 Antitrust laws, or unfair competition laws, are designed to prevent the restriction of competition between businesses; for example, when only one company is responsible for the supply of a country's telephone services. How can a monopoly such as this affect other businesses?

2 Some countries introduce regulations in order to protect their domestic industries from foreign competition. What are some of the pros and cons of such protectionist practices?

3 Which mergers can you think of between large international corporations in the last five years? Have they all been successful? What problems have been encountered?

READING

A Understanding the main points

Read the article on the opposite page and answer these questions.

1 Why is InBev's acquisition of Anheuser-Busch of particular interest to any company thinking of making a business acquisition in China?

2 Which Chinese domestic industry is being protected by the measures taken by Mofcom, and exactly how are these Chinese companies being protected?

B Understanding details

1 **Read the article again and answer these questions.**

  1 Had there already been a published decision relating to the new anti-monopoly laws in China, prior to the one described in the article?
  2 Why was InBev's takeover of Anheuser-Busch allowed?
  3 Which countries are these two companies based in?
  4 Why exactly did the acquisition need Mofcom's consent?
  5 When allowing the acquisition, Mofcom imposed a number of restrictions. Were these restrictions expected?
  6 What effects do the Mofcom restrictions have on InBev?
  7 Which two Chinese companies does InBev now have shares in?
  8 What message is Erik Söderlind sending out to company leaders?
  9 What is the unusual aspect of this Mofcom decision, so that future acquisitions by foreign companies might be approached differently?

InBev ruling sparks fears for M&A in China

by Sundeep Tucker

A The first published ruling by China's new antitrust regime has led to fears that authorities could use the laws to protect domestic industry from foreign competition.

B In November, China's Ministry of Commerce (Mofcom) waved through InBev's $52bn acquisition of Anheuser-Busch on the grounds that it would not adversely affect competition in the domestic beer market. It is the first publication of a merger decision since strengthened anti-monopoly laws took effect in August.

C The high-profile global deal required Chinese approval because Belgium-based InBev and Anheuser-Busch of the US generated large enough sales on the mainland to justify an investigation.

D However, in a single-page ruling, Mofcom also imposed a number of unanticipated restrictions that will prevent InBev acquiring further interests in four key companies in the Chinese beer market.

E Lawyers said that, by imposing future conditions on a deal that did not harm competition, Mofcom had broken new ground in international antitrust decision-making. This is likely to alter the approach of many overseas companies towards mergers and acquisitions in China, they believe.

F The ruling states that InBev cannot increase Anheuser-Busch's existing 27 per cent shareholding in Tsingtao Brewery or its own 28.5 per cent stake in Zhujiang Brewery.

G Mofcom also banned InBev from acquiring shares in two other big domestic breweries, China Resources Snow and Beijing Yanjing. InBev will also have to inform Mofcom 'in a timely manner' of any changes to its controlling shareholders.

H Erik Söderlind, law firm Linklaters' Asia Head of Competition, said: 'As a result of the InBev ruling, company bosses considering M&A will now have to take into account the risk that a Chinese antitrust ruling on one transaction can impose restrictions on their ability to do future deals on the mainland.'

FT

2 **Read the article again and say whether these statements are true (T) or false (F). Correct the false ones.**

1 China is still operating a long-established set of antitrust laws.
2 The Mofcom decision was recorded in a lengthy document.
3 InBev must give up its part-ownership of Zhujiang Brewery.
4 InBev is obliged to tell Mofcom if any of its main shareholders change.
5 Erik Söderlind believes that this Mofcom ruling could be repeated for future foreign mergers and acquisitions.

VOCABULARY

A Word search

1 **Find words or phrases in the article which have similar meanings.**

1 decision from the court (paragraph A)

r........

2 allowed (usually without much delay or questioning) (paragraph B)

w........t........

3 for the reason that (paragraph B)

o........t........g........t........

4 regulations to prevent one company controlling a market (paragraph B)

a........-m........l........

5 financial shares in a company (paragraph D)

i........

6 done something new, original, pioneering (paragraph E)

b........n........g........

7 within reasonable time, in good time (paragraph G)

in a t........m........

2 **Find words or phrases in the article which fit these meanings.**

1 a commonly used business abbreviation for mergers and acquisitions (title)
2 have a negative effect on (paragraph B)
3 an international agreement that has had a lot of attention (paragraph C)
4 consent, agreement (paragraph C)
5 put in place several unexpected limitations (paragraph D)
6 important, significant (paragraph D)
7 when companies come together to form one organisation, and when one company takes over another (paragraph E)
8 a financial interest in a company (two words) (paragraph F)
9 prohibited (paragraph G)

B Word partnerships

Match these words to make verb–noun partnerships. Some nouns can go with more than one verb. Check your answers in a dictionary.

to suffer	
to block	a decision
to veto	a proposal
to overturn	a defeat
to uphold	

ILEC **C** **Text completion**

Choose the best word to fill the gap from the choices A–D below the extract.

EU to pay damages over merger deal veto

by Tobias Buck and Pan Kwan Yuk

Brussels' competition regulator recently suffered an embarrassing legal defeat that saw it, for the first time, ordered to pay ....[1] for wrongly blocking a European merger.

The European Court of First Instance ruled that the European Commission was ....[2] of 'a grave and manifest disregard' for the limits of its power when it blocked the proposed €6.7bn merger of Schneider Electric and Legrand, two French electrical equipment makers.

Schneider Electric had demanded €1.66bn in ....[3] for the losses arising from a 2001 European Commission ruling vetoing its merger with rival group Legrand.

When the merger was vetoed, Schneider already had 98 per cent of Legrand's shares and subsequently divested the shareholding at a ....[4] to satisfy the EU regulators.

The ruling was ....[5] one year later, after the European Court of First Instance, the EU's second-highest court, found the Commission had committed grave errors in assessing the tie-up.

The same court later ruled that the regulator's mistakes were so serious that Schneider deserved compensation. It did not, however, ...[6] the group's full claim, saying it was in part to blame for the losses.

The court has never before ....[7] damages arising from EU merger or antitrust decisions, so the decision is likely to encourage other groups in similar situations to follow suit. The ruling also serves as a powerful reminder to the Commission that the court is not afraid to inflict both embarrassment and financial harm on the regulator if it fails to uphold companies' rights.

FT

	A	B	C	D
1	money	damage	penalty	damages
2	liable	guilty	innocent	ordered
3	rebate	discount	compensation	punishment
4	loss	market	profit	cost
5	suppressed	refused	deleted	overturned
6	state	uphold	declare	maintain
7	awarded	specified	given	inflicted

OVER TO YOU

1. Do you think commercial enterprises have a right to expect their governments to provide a degree of protection so that businesses stay active and continue to provide jobs? Or will this simply lead to lack of true competition and a slow-down in genuine technical development? Discuss this with a colleague or write an essay stating your views.
2. To what extent should business activities be monitored by a government, to ensure they are carried out in a fair and proper manner? Should some sectors be especially closely controlled? For example, the financial sector? And how should the monitoring bodies themselves be evaluated for effectiveness and professionalism? Discuss this with a colleague or write an essay stating your views.

UNIT 8

Cybercrime – a worldwide threat

This unit looks at the rapidly growing problem of cybercrime – using computers and the Internet to obtain confidential information, or to trick members of the public.

BEFORE YOU READ

Discuss these questions.

1 Fraudulent e-mails are ones which aim to cheat people. What examples of these dishonest e-mails can you think of? Do you know anyone who has received one?

2 What can companies do to protect sensitive data on their computer files from being accessed by hackers? How can the police help?

3 Do cybercriminals have any special skills that the business world could benefit from? If so, how could these skills be used in a legitimate way?

READING

A Understanding the main points

1 **Read the article on the opposite page and answer these questions.**

1 Why does the writer use Mr Ericson's story at the start of the article?
2 What progress are companies making in fighting cybercrime?

2 **Which of the following cybercrime-related matters are mentioned in the article?**

1 high-level police investigations to prevent cybercrime
2 misuse of company trademarks and patents
3 hacking into government computer networks
4 fraudulent e-mails
5 credit-card fraud

B Understanding details

Read the article again and answer these questions.

1 Why did Mr Ericson believe he really had won a prize?
2 What did he have to pay for in order to receive the prize money?
3 What action has Microsoft taken to deal with cybercrime?
4 What is *phishing*?
5 How does RSA's Internet network help banks?
6 What is the purpose of a 'take-down' letter?
7 Why are companies encouraged to keep records of cybercrimes?
8 Which particular situation is highlighted when Microsoft advises companies to inform their customers if there is a scam?

Investigators take on the cybercrooks

by Maija Palmer

A Tom Ericson did not think he was the kind of person who could easily be tricked. But the 68-year-old Scandinavian, whose long international business 5 career included working for a large multinational bank, recently lost thousands of dollars to a lottery scam, an illegal activity aiming to cheat people.

B Mr Ericson received an e-mail, 10 apparently from Microsoft, which informed him that the company's lottery fund had picked him as the winner of a major prize. He was delighted. The Microsoft name reassured him, and his 15 telephone call to the number given in the e-mail was handled in a professional manner. He was told a cheque would be posted to him straightaway.

C There was just the matter of a 20 handling fee to pay first, which Mr Ericson did by Western Union. Then there was a tax charge, a $14,600 security deposit and legal fees. But no prize money was released.

D Mr Ericson became suspicious and went to the police. They referred the case to Microsoft's internal investigation department, which tracks lottery scams in a more systematic way than 30 many police forces are able to. 'We investigate every single lead and try to build cases from them,' says Peter Anaman, a former French army officer who now works as a cybercrime investigator 35 at Microsoft.

E The US software giant is not the only business developing an online policing role. An increasing number of companies are becoming proactive in tracking 40 down cybercriminals who abuse their trademarks, disrupt their businesses and prey on their customers.

F Microsoft has about 65 investigators and lawyers working full time on 45 tracking cybercrime. PayPal, the online payments service, has a similar number. Some banks, such as HSBC, also invest heavily in in-house teams. Other companies seeking protection may pay 50 six- or seven-figure sums for Internet security specialists to provide something similar to a private detective service.

G RSA, the Internet security specialist, for example, works for most of the 55 world's largest banks to identify and stop phishing attempts, in which e-mails claiming to be from trusted contacts encourage victims to hand over confidential data. RSA runs an interna- 60 tional network through which more than 2,500 banks can quickly share information about cybercrime attacks.

H So what practical action are companies taking? Microsoft's investigators 65 compile information about the scammers, then hand their files over to the police, who carry out any arrests. Microsoft has to date supported 550 public and private prosecutions. 'Some 70 people have been locked away, and in some cases the criminal activity has stopped altogether. It's moving forward in the right direction,' says Mr Anaman.

I **When brands are threatened**

75 Microsoft has some words of advice for companies that discover their names used in Internet scams:

1. Alert your legal department, which can then notify the national law 80 enforcement body, preferably the national cybercrime unit. They will be in a position to communicate with Europol and Interpol.
2. Send a 'take-down' letter to the Inter- 85 net service provider requesting the closure of the sender's e-mail account and any e-mail accounts mentioned in the body of the scam.
3. Keep records of the reports and scams 90 received in order to be in a better position to evaluate the threat and share the results of your investigations with the national law enforcement body.
4. 95 Consider warning your customers about the scam through the company website, especially if your business is not usually targeted by fraudsters.

FT

VOCABULARY

A Understanding expressions

Choose the best explanation for each phrase from the article.

1 'Investigators *take on the cybercrooks*' (title)
   a) arrest cheating e-mailers
   b) are ready to fight cybercriminals
2 '... *apparently* from Microsoft ...' (line 10)
   a) definitely
   b) seeming to be
3 'The Microsoft name *reassured him* ...' (lines 13–14)
   a) made him feel it was a genuine e-mail
   b) warned him it may be a trick
4 'Mr Ericson *became suspicious* ...' (line 25)
   a) thought maybe something was wrong
   b) knew he had been cheated
5 '... which *tracks* lottery scams ...' (lines 28–29)
   a) follows the progress of
   b) prevents
6 '... and *prey on their customers*.' (lines 41–42)
   a) make customers victims
   b) contact customers without permission
7 'Microsoft has *to date* supported ...' (line 68)
   a) in total
   b) up to now
8 'Some people have been *locked away* ...' (lines 69–70)
   a) moved out of their jobs
   b) put in prison

B Legal terminology

Find words or phrases in paragraphs D–I of the article which fit these meanings.

1 an adjective meaning you have doubts about the honesty of someone or something
2 organisations of policemen and women
3 a clue which may help solve a crime
4 an investigator who does not work for the police
5 people who suffer the effects of a crime
6 put together information (e.g. to solve a crime)
7 when the police hold people they believe are criminals
8 the name for legal proceedings in a criminal court

C Sentence completion

Use words or phrases from Exercise B in the correct form to complete these sentences.

1 Many people have been tricked by e-mail scams – there have been .... all over the world.

2 The police have made several ...., which have resulted in successful .... These people are now in prison.

3 She was a little .... about the way the man on the train kept looking at her handbag. Did he want to steal it?

4 The security people had .... a detailed list of all e-mails received in the last six months.

5 He used to be a member of one of the biggest .... in the country. After he retired, he became a ....

6 So far, there have been absolutely no .... The police have no idea who stole the diamonds, or even when they were stolen.

D Vocabulary development

1 **Read paragraph I of the article again and answer these questions.**

1 Scams are carried out by scammers. Which word is used for people who carry out frauds?

2 What are the two different uses of the word *body* in sections 1 and 2 of Microsoft's advice?

3 Give two synonyms for the word *evaluate* in section 3.

4 Section 4 refers to a business being *targeted*. What exactly is a *target*, and why is this verb used here?

2 **Think of words to fit these meanings, then check your answers in paragraph I.**

1 to give information to, to tell n........

2 a four-word expression meaning 'a country's police force' n........ l........ e........ b........

3 the act of closing something down c........

4 think about doing something c........

OVER TO YOU

1 An older relative of yours has just started using the Internet and sending e-mails. Draw up a list of steps he or she should take to protect against scams and hacking, pointing out any signs from incoming e-mails that should put your relative on the alert.

2 Communication technology has radically altered business life in the last 20 years – some things have improved, but, as we have seen, there is now a whole new range of problems. Prepare for a discussion on the pros and cons of new technology, particularly in relation to how the business world might be without it.

3 Crime is really a matter for the police, and so-called 'cybercrime' is no exception. Companies should not have to give up valuable time and resources doing police work. After all, police forces are financed from taxes raised from companies. Give a five-minute presentation either for or against this view, using examples to support your opinion.

UNIT 9

Protecting intellectual property

This unit illustrates how commercial organisations face the problem of having their products copied and sold without their permission, an offence commonly known as *piracy* or *counterfeiting*.

BEFORE YOU READ

Discuss these questions.

1 Have you seen counterfeit goods offered for sale? What type of goods were they, and how did they differ from the original product?

2 IP (intellectual property) rights relate to 'intangible' assets (that is, assets that cannot be touched, that are not physical). The design of packaging and labelling is one example. What are other examples?

3 What are the possible commercial consequences suffered by a company if another company begins to market cheap copies of its products, particularly if the products have a reputation for good quality? Think of different types of product that are typically pirated.

READING

A Understanding the main points

Read the article on the opposite page and say whether these statements are true (T) or false (F). Correct the false ones.

1 This was the first time Diageo had complained about the copying of its whisky-bottle design and packaging.

2 The award of damages made by the Shanghai court was a standard sum for a case of this nature.

3 This case shows that the Chinese authorities have been taking piracy issues seriously for some years now.

4 Chinese companies do not take legal action because they think the courts will not support them.

5 Beijing and Shanghai courts are considered to be more effective at enforcing their decisions than other courts in China.

B Understanding meaning

Choose the best explanation for these ideas from the article.

1 '... as part of *a government crackdown on rampant piracy*.' (lines 5–6)

a) strong government action being taken against ever-increasing acts of piracy
b) new government regulations against different forms of piracy

2 '... comes in the *midst* of a [...] campaign ...' (lines 16–18)

a) confusion
b) middle

3 '... intellectual property protection is a *perennial issue* ...' (lines 29–30)

a) constant point of discussion
b) bargaining tool

Chinese authorities take counterfeiting seriously

by Jamil Anderlini

A A Shanghai court has ordered a Chinese company to pay Rmb1.25m ($183,000) in damages to British drinks group Diageo for copying its packaging as part of a government crackdown on rampant piracy.

B The court found that Blueblood (Shanghai) Wine copied the bottle design and packaging of Diageo's popular Johnnie Walker Black Label whisky for its own brand of whisky, Polonius, and continued to do so even after being fined by the Shanghai government, following a previous complaint from Diageo. The award is unusually high and comes in the midst of a Shanghai government anti-piracy campaign, in which officials are trying to show their commitment to protecting intellectual property rights.

C Lawyers who specialise in intellectual property cases say the Diageo ruling, although clearly part of a propaganda offensive, does signal the Chinese authorities are taking counterfeiting much more seriously than in previous years. China is the biggest source of counterfeit goods in the world, and intellectual property protection is a perennial issue at trade negotiations and diplomatic exchanges with other countries.

D In Diageo's case the Chinese company copied packaging rather than any registered patent, copyright or trademark, and the guilty verdict signalled a greater level of sophistication from the courts than most previous rulings, lawyers said.

E Chinese courts dealt with over 17,000 intellectual property cases last year, compared with just over 400 handled by courts in the UK in the same period. The vast majority of cases in China involve local companies suing other local companies, as Chinese businessmen become increasingly willing to use the law to protect intangible assets.

F But companies that win court cases in China often have difficulty getting the rulings enforced. 'Generally speaking, enforcement is still a big issue, especially outside the major centres of Beijing and Shanghai,' according to Luke Minford, Head of China for Rouse, the intellectual property consultancy. 'Most foreign companies will try to get their case heard in Shanghai and Beijing in order to get more sophisticated and objective judges, but trying to enforce in other areas is still very difficult.'

G On the same day as the Diageo ruling, the Shanghai court handed down verdicts on 13 other cases, nine of which involved international companies, including 3M, Nippon Electric, New Zealand kiwifruit company Zespri and Rock Records, a Taiwanese record label, state media reported.

FT

4 '... the guilty verdict *signalled a greater level of sophistication* ...' (lines 36–37)

a) showed things had developed and improved

b) indicated things must develop and improve

5 '... the Shanghai court *handed down* verdicts on 13 other cases ...' (lines 64–65)

a) listened to

b) gave decisions on

VOCABULARY

A Legal terminology

1 **Find words or phrases in the article which fit these meanings.**

1 making illegal copies (title)
2 financial compensation awarded by a court (paragraph A)
3 punished by having to pay a money penalty (paragraph B)
4 rights which relate to non-physical, or intangible, assets (paragraph B)
5 three examples of intangible assets (paragraph D)
6 court decision that someone is not innocent (paragraph D)
7 taking legal action in a civil (as opposed to criminal) court (paragraph E)
8 making sure that court orders are carried out (paragraph F)

2 **Decide which word does not fit in each group.**

1 damages / compensation / complaint
2 piracy / theft / counterfeiting
3 court / fine / sentence
4 product / trademark / copyright
5 ruling / statement / decision
6 sue / prosecute / enforce

B Sentence completion

Use the words or phrases from Exercise A to complete these sentences. Note that you may need to change the word form (e.g. verb to noun/adjective).

1 The song had the same tune as a hit from the 1980s; the original publishers claimed substantial .... in court.
2 For an offence like that, you can receive a very heavy ....
3 It's no use just asking them to stop using that packaging – we'll have to threaten to .... them before they'll take any notice.
4 For patent registrations, we need to speak to lawyers specialising in ....
5 These $20 notes are .... The store refused to accept them.
6 The court ruling was in the manufacturer's favour. Now it's a question of making sure that the ruling is ....
7 The .... handed down by the court caused bad publicity and affected the sales of the company almost immediately.
8 A .... is a particular name or symbol that has been registered by a company and so cannot be used by anyone else.

ILEC **C**

Text completion

Choose the best word to fill the gap from the choices A–D below the extract.

Rise in cases to protect companies' copyright

by Jonathan Moules

Intellectual ....[1] lawyers are warning of a jump in court cases involving patents, trademarks and ....[2] as the economy worsens.

5 The number of ....[3] is already on the rise, increasing 83 per cent last year, according to the latest judicial statistics, as business owners become more aware of the need to protect 10 their ideas.

Tom Farrand, Director of Trademarks at IP21, an intellectual property advisory service, said he had seen a sharp increase in inquiries during the 15 past few months from companies looking to ....[4] designs. 'During a downturn, companies start looking over their shoulder and enforce their ....[5] against others, rather than tak- 20 ing a forward-looking attitude and asking what new products they can launch,' he said.

The biggest increase was in claims over 'passing off', the ....[6] use of a 25 style, look or brand associated with another company, followed by infringement of trademark cases. Patents and registered design claims rose 95 per cent, while copyright and 30 design right cases were up 43 per cent.

FT

	A	B	C	D
1	patent	activity	property	ownership
2	logos	copywrite	packaging	copyright
3	regulations	claims	verdicts	damages
4	prevent	produce	predict	protect
5	positions	cases	rights	losses
6	unauthorised	competitive	distinctive	licensed

D

Vocabulary development

Choose the correct intellectual property term for each definition.

1 Manufacturing a product so it looks very similar to an existing product, so that customers are cheated, is known as ....

a) passing off b) putting off

2 Illegally copying a trademark, patent or copyrighted material is called ....

a) falsification b) infringement

OVER TO YOU

1 You know someone who is just starting his own small business making a range of bottled sauces for food. He knows about cooking, but he has not thought much yet about the implications of a good product name, a slogan, the design of the label, etc. Write a short report (250–300 words) explaining what he should be aware of from a legal point of view and highlighting the risks of another company copying his products.

2 Find out about a court case in your country involving counterfeit goods or another intellectual property rights issue, and explain it to a colleague in your own words. Include the court's decision in your explanation.

UNIT 10

New ways of dealing with fraud

This unit looks at a report on how law firms are tackling the problem of fraud.

BEFORE YOU READ

Discuss these questions.

1 Why is fraud becoming a growing problem internationally? What can lawyers do to deal with this increase?
2 Price-fixing is one kind of fraud. Can you think of others that can affect businesses?
3 The 'fraud squad' – the main police fraud office in various countries – is well known from films and TV crime series. How can anti-fraud agencies in different countries work together to fight crime?

READING

A Understanding the main points

Read the article on the opposite page and answer these questions.

1 In the first example, involving the firm Peters & Peters, in what ways did the prosecutors and the defendants benefit from the outcome of the case?
2 How did the two other law firms earn themselves a mention in the 'fraud section' of the report?

ILEC B Understanding details

Read the article again and choose the best answer (A, B, C or D) to these questions.

1 What does paragraph A say about 'marine hoses'?
   A They were first used in December last year.
   B A lot of criminals knew about them.
   C They are now known to some lawyers involved in financial cases.
   D They are pipes used in the navy.
2 In paragraph C, what were the three men found guilty of?
   A Criminal offences which they had committed in the UK
   B Stealing the marine hoses from ships
   C Being part of a conspiracy to fix the prices of the hoses
   D Being part of a conspiracy to use the hoses to steal crude oil
3 Why was the US Department of Justice pleased with the case?
   A Because the Department now feels other countries will be encouraged to make price-fixing laws more effective.
   B Because the case was conducted in a vigorous, lively manner.
   C Because the Department is very ambitious.
   D Because the case fitted well with the kind of law the Department is interested in.

Thinking about fraud

by Michael Peel

Globalisation of fraud and the expansion in cross-border investigations mean lawyers have to think in more dimensions than ever before

A Few people outside the highly specialised world of oil-industry logistics had heard of marine hoses before they were the subject of a landmark price-fixing case in December last year. Now the pipes have become famous – at least in the world of financial crime prevention, even though they still may not be more widely known about.

B The reason is that under a deal put together by Peters & Peters (one of the top firms in the section on fraud in the *Financial Times* report 'Innovative Lawyers'), the hoses were the reason for the UK's first criminal cartel case and a groundbreaking transatlantic deal between competition authorities.

C Under the agreement, three men – two of whom were represented by Peters & Peters – pleaded guilty in the US to their involvement in a long-running conspiracy to fix the prices of the hoses, which are used to transfer crude oil between storage vessels. In exchange, the men were allowed to travel to the UK to admit to similar offences and serve prison sentences there.

D The trio – known as 'the marine-hose three', following the 'NatWest three' case involving three British bankers convicted of fraud in the US – were sentenced to between 30 and 36 months in jail each in June. Lawyers say the deal was clever because it worked for both the prosecutors and the defence, suggesting it could be used in other financial crime cases with a transatlantic dimension.

E The UK's Office of Fair Trading was delighted to have its first criminal cartel trial run so smoothly, while the case fitted in with the US Department of Justice's ambition of encouraging other countries to enforce price-fixing laws more vigorously. For the defendants, the agreement meant they could serve their sentences nearer home and benefit from the UK's more generous parole rules.

F Other leading entries in the fraud section of the Financial Times report have similarly wide implications at a time of great change in financial crime laws and their enforcement.

G CMS Cameron McKenna's 'Fighting Fraud Together' programme is an attempt to help break down the long-standing mutual suspicions between the authorities and the private sector that restrict the sharing of information useful in tackling fraud. The firm oversaw the sharing of mortgage fraud information between institutions and the police in an attempt to recover millions of pounds of losses and catch the perpetrators.

H DLA Piper cast its net even wider in its initiative to help companies comply with regulations globally by using web-based applications and questionnaires to profile risk and identify shortcomings.

I The existence of a fraud section in the report – like the marine-hose-three deal itself – is a sign of how the globalisation of fraud and the expansion in cross-border investigations means lawyers in the field are having to think in more dimensions than ever before.

FT

4 What was the advantage of the case outcome for the 'marine-hose three'?

A They did not have to go to prison in the US.
B They received a reduced prison sentence.
C They were released and allowed to go home.
D They received generous payments from the UK.

5 What is the aim of the 'Fighting Fraud Together' campaign?

A To help the police catch criminals quickly
B To encourage public authorities and private industry to work together against fraud
C To identify suspicious people who may be guilty of fraud
D To allow lawyers to get more information from the police

6 What does the writer conclude is needed as a result of growing international fraud?

A More careful cross-border investigations
B More lawyers working out in the field
C Increasing use of the Internet to detect fraud
D Lawyers having to consider fraud cases in fresh and different ways

VOCABULARY

A Understanding expressions

Choose the best explanation for each phrase from the article.

1 '... the subject of a *landmark* price-fixing case ...' (lines 8–9)
   a) belonging to one country
   b) significant, especially for future decisions

2 '... the [...] report "*Innovative Lawyers*" ...' (lines 16–18)
   a) creative, inventive lawyers
   b) financially successful lawyers

3 '... between *competition authorities*.' (line 21)
   a) different government bodies that compete with each other
   b) official organisations that control unfair competition issues

4 '... a long-running *conspiracy* ...' (lines 25–26)
   a) crime committed at sea; similar to piracy
   b) agreement between parties to do something unlawful

5 '... its first *criminal cartel* trial ...' (line 45–46)
   a) an illegal association of companies that agree, e.g. to fix prices
   b) a document which is evidence of an illegal agreement between companies

6 '... to *enforce* [...] *laws more vigorously*.' (lines 49–50)
   a) try harder to make sure laws are obeyed
   b) force more people to obey the law

7 '... the UK's more generous *parole* rules.' (lines 53–54)
   a) official standard of living conditions in prison
   b) release from prison, subject to certain restrictions

8 '... between *the authorities and the private sector* ...' (lines 63–64)
   a) the police and private investigators
   b) government organisations and commercial organisations

9 '... catch the *perpetrators*.' (lines 70–71)
   a) people who commit a crime
   b) escaped prisoners

B Word partnerships

Match the verbs (1–7) with the nouns (a–g) to form common word partnerships often found in legal or commercial contexts.

1 to put together	a) a crime
2 to plead	b) a prison sentence
3 to fix	c) losses
4 to serve	d) a deal
5 to be convicted of	e) regulations
6 to recover	f) guilty
7 to comply with	g) prices

C Sentence completion

Use the word partnerships from Exercise B in the correct form to complete these sentences.

1 At the court hearing, the accused .... to the charge of theft.
2 It is illegal for different companies to agree to .... the .... of products that they all sell.
3 He was found guilty of insurance fraud and had to .... of three years.
4 The company was not able to .... all the .... they suffered as a result of the fraud.
5 Lawyers for the company being offered for sale .... a very attractive .... for the prospective purchasers.
6 Every year, there are more and more .... for small businesses to ....
7 The application form had a section where you had to say if you had been ....

ILEC D Word families

Use the words on the right so they fit into the sentences correctly.

1	The supplier and the company entered into an	**agree**
2	He was found guilty of a criminal	**offend**
3	He has had two criminal	**convict**
4	One principal task of the police is law	**enforce**
5	The new law is intended to .... telephone selling.	**regulation**
6	We failed to .... with the tax requirements.	**compliance**

E Prepositions

Complete these sentences using the correct prepositions.

1 The man was convicted .... dangerous driving.
2 The woman was sentenced .... six months .... prison .... shoplifting.
3 In court, he did not admit .... previous offences.
4 Both company directors pleaded guilty .... the charge .... discrimination.
5 It is essential to comply .... the new labelling regulations.

OVER TO YOU

1 What can be the effects of price-fixing on business in general? Who exactly can suffer as a result? Discuss with a colleague and list your ideas.

2 Do you think it is a good idea for lawyers to be 'creative', as described in the article, or should they stick to advising on the law as it stands? Give a short presentation or write a summary of your views.

3 We have seen how lawyers have shown innovation in the area of financial crime. What other areas of law lend themselves to this innovative approach? Think about this, then visit the *Financial Times* website and view the 'Innovative Lawyers' Report.

UNIT 11

The costs of pollution

This unit looks at how environmental legislation can have a significant impact on existing businesses.

BEFORE YOU READ

Discuss these questions.

1 You run a large manufacturing plant which has been operating, largely unchanged, for about 10 years. You produce items of heavy machinery for use in factories. What parts of your manufacturing process might need updating as a result of strict new anti-pollution laws? How could these changes impact on your business financially?

2 In what way are the environmental responsibilities of companies different from, say, 30 or 40 years ago? In particular, think about the petroleum industry, drilling for oil and transporting it.

READING

A Understanding the main points

Read the articles on the opposite page and answer these questions.

Article 1

1 What does BusinessEurope fear will happen to some manufacturing plants? And why will this happen?

2 What is the relevance of the IPPC directive?

Article 2

3 What is the connection between Texaco Petroleum and Chevron?

4 What is the relevance of the 1989 oil spill from the tanker Exxon Valdez?

B Understanding details

Read the articles again and answer these questions.

Article 1

1 Which directives are the EU proposals aimed at?

2 If governments do not meet anti-pollution targets, what could the result be?

3 What would BusinessEurope like to see industry do instead of cutting production?

4 Which two areas of flexibility does BusinessEurope believe governments might lose?

5 Why did the European Commission give its support to Stavros Dimas's proposal?

6 Why is existing environmental legislation not easy to administer?

Article 2

7 What kind of record might be set by this legal action?

8 What kind of suit have lawyers brought against Chevron?

9 What is the nature of the claim made against Chevron?

10 What action did Texaco take to improve the situation after it left in 1992?

Article 1

Industry threatened by EU pollution law

by Andrew Bounds

A Plans to tighten European Union anti-pollution legislation could force the closure of large numbers of industries, business leaders have warned.

B The European Commission put forward proposals just before Christmas to toughen directives dealing with dust, sulphur and nitrogen emissions that cause acid rain and smog, saying that national governments were set to miss reduction targets that could save tens of thousands of lives.

C However, BusinessEurope, which represents employers across the EU, says that the high cost of compliance could force many plants to shut down. 'These directives will impose a disproportionate cost on industry, leading to production cuts in Europe rather than to to further innovation and investment in clean technologies,' it said in a letter to commissioners involved in the legislation.

D Crucially, it said, governments' right to allow flexibility according to the location and design of power stations, steel mills and the like would be taken away. The Commission believes this right has been abused to give polluters too much flexibility and wants them to justify any departure from the list of mitigation measures.

E Governments have fallen behind schedule and have only assessed half of eligible plants for compliance with the Integrated Pollution Prevention Control directive (IPPC). So Stavros Dimas, the Environment Commissioner, won Commission backing – after fierce internal debate – for his proposal to tighten standards and gather seven anti-pollution measures in a single, reorganised Industrial Emissions directive. 'The way environmental legislation has grown has been to regulate one substance at a time. That makes it very complicated to administer. So we have proposed simplifying things,' said his spokeswoman.

F In the BusinessEurope letter, Philippe de Buck, Secretary-General, asked Günter Verheugen, Industry Commissioner, that new proposals for national emission ceilings be 'realistic' and not involve measures that go beyond the IPPC system.

G However, green groups welcomed the proposals and called on national governments and the European parliament not to block them.

Article 2

Chevron to contest Ecuador pollution lawsuit

by Naomi Mapstone

A The stretch of Amazon jungle on Ecuador's border with Colombia is marked with long, deep pits of black oil and earth. Over 900 pits were used by Texaco Petroleum of the US and by PetroEcuador, the state company, for the 23 years before Texaco left the country in 1992.

B Now they are at the centre of what is becoming the biggest environmental lawsuit in history, with $27bn in potential damages sought against Chevron, which bought Texaco in 2001. That is almost seven times the damages awarded against ExxonMobil for the 1989 Exxon Valdez oil-tanker spill in Alaska.

C The fact that this rough, poor frontier land is heavily polluted is not at issue. But after 15 years of litigation, almost every other aspect of the case is contested. Lawyers who brought the class action suit against Chevron say Texaco operated below environmental standards of the day to maximise profits.

D Chevron, the world's third-biggest oil company, denies the charges. It says its responsibility ended when it cleaned up 37.5 per cent of the well sites as part of a $40m remediation agreement with the Ecuadorean government in 1995. PetroEcuador, Texaco's consortium partner, which continues to operate in Lago Agrio, has responsibility for the remaining sites, it argues. PetroEcuador declined to comment.

VOCABULARY

A Legal terminology

1 **Find words or phrases in the articles which fit these meanings.**

Article 1

1 to make laws stricter (paragraph A)
2 formal suggestions, usually made by a committee (paragraph B)
3 EU laws (paragraph B)
4 steps that can be taken to prevent pollution (paragraph E)
5 laws relating to the environment (paragraph E)
6 top limits for emissions (paragraph F)

Article 2

7 not disputed (paragraph C)
8 not accepted (paragraph C)
9 a law case on behalf of a group of people (paragraph C)
10 says it does not admit claims against it (paragraph D)
11 an arrangement to pay money to put things right (paragraph D)
12 said nothing in response to claims and allegations (paragraph D)

2 **Decide which word does not fit in each group.**

1 law / verdict / directive
2 misuse / ignore / abuse
3 instruct / control / regulate
4 lawsuit / case / arbitration
5 deny / allege / admit
6 comply with / obey / enforce

B Word partnerships

1 **Match the verbs (1–5) with the nouns (a–d). Some nouns can be used with more than one verb.**

1 to put forward	a) standards
2 to toughen	b) rights
3 to abuse	c) proposals
4 to tighten	d) laws
5 to block	

2 **Look through Article 1 and underline the six word partnerships from Exercise 1 that are used. Sometimes the noun in the article may be slightly different (e.g. *directives* instead of *laws*) and sometimes the word partnership may be split by other words in the same sentence.**

C Vocabulary development

to mitigate, mitigation, mitigating

In court, to *mitigate* means 'to reduce the seriousness of a charge'.
In general business, it means 'to reduce' (for example, a company can take action to mitigate losses).

1 **Match these expressions (1–3) with their meanings (a–c).**

1 mitigating circumstances	a) a reduction in the amount of compensation awarded
2 a plea in mitigation	b) factors which make a crime less serious
3 mitigation of damages	c) a response to a charge, aiming to reduce a sentence

2 **Choose the correct meaning of *mitigation measures* (Article 1, line 32).**

a) methods which will reduce pollution
b) steps to reduce the strict application of anti-pollution laws

ILEC D Word families

Use the words on the right so they fit into the phrases correctly. Then look back at the articles on page 45 to check your answers.

Article 1

1 ... the high cost of .... could ... (lines 15–16)	**to comply**
2 These directives will .... a disproportionate cost ... (lines 17–18)	**imposition**
3 ... have only assessed half of .... plants ... (lines 34–35)	**eligibility**
4 So Stavros Dimas [...] won Commission .... (lines 37–39)	**a backer**

Article 2

5 ... this [...] land is heavily .... (lines 18–19)	**pollution**
6 Lawyers who brought the class action .... against ... (lines 22–23)	**to sue**
7 ... Texaco operated [...] to .... profits. (lines 23–25)	**maximum**
8 ... as part of a $40m .... agreement ... (lines 29–30)	**remedy**

OVER TO YOU

1 Many governments introduce new regulations in the name of caring for the environment, but do all these laws really make a difference? Provide arguments supporting whatever views you have about the effectiveness of the state's role in environmental protection.

2 What measures have you read or heard about that you think could be introduced in your country to encourage the business community to adopt environmentally friendly practices? Do you think large international corporations have a greater responsibility than small businesses? If so, what role should they take?

UNIT 12

A safe workplace?

This unit looks at an extract from the Health and Safety at Work Act 1974, the principal legislation that governs how employers in the UK should provide their employees with a safe environment to work in.

BEFORE YOU READ

Discuss these questions.

1 Which laws in your country relate to the health and safety of employees at work? Are they strictly enforced? Are all employers fully aware of their legal responsibilities in this area?

2 What responsibility should employees take for their own health and safety? Is there a risk that 'protecting' laws and regulations can take away an individual's sense of responsibility for his or her own actions?

3 What key health and safety factors can you think of that are relevant a) for employees working in a large factory, and b) for those working in an office block? Name five or six in each case.

READING

A Understanding the main points

Read Section 2 of the Act on the opposite page and answer these questions.

1 What is the main topic of Section 2 of the Health and Safety at Work Act 1974?

2 Choose the correct name for the different numbered parts the section is divided into.

a) divisions b) subsections c) paragraphs d) clauses

3 Why is there no Section 2(5)?

B Understanding details

Read Section 2 of the Act again and answer these questions.

1 What does Section 2(2)c relate to?

a) transport of articles and substances
b) training and supervision
c) proper maintenance of a place of work

2 Which part of Section 2(2) contains a reference to the employees' working environment?

3 Look at Section 2(3). What are the main duties of an employer in respect of a company health and safety policy?

4 What is the principal function of the safety committee as described in Section 2(7)?

5 Which subsection relates to the appointment of safety representatives by trade unions? Are those representatives from outside the company?

6 Subsections 2(1) to 2(3) of the original 1974 Act were changed by later legislation. Which regulations brought about the change? What does the modification of the subsections specifically relate to?

Health and Safety at Work Act 1974

(Section 2 – general duties)

2 General duties of employers to their employees

(1) It shall be the duty of every employer to ensure, so far as is reasonably practicable, the health, safety and welfare at work of all his employees.

(2) Without prejudice to the generality of an employer's duty under the preceding subsection, the matters to which that duty extends include in particular:

(a) the provision and maintenance of plant and systems of work that are, so far as is reasonably practicable, safe and without risks to health;

(b) arrangements for ensuring, so far as is reasonably practicable, safety and absence of risks to health in connection with the use, handling, storage and transport of articles and substances;

(c) the provision of such information, instruction, training and supervision as is necessary to ensure, so far as is reasonably practicable, the health and safety at work of his employees;

(d) so far as is reasonably practicable as regards any place of work under the employer's control, the maintenance of it in a condition that is safe and without risks to health and the provision and maintenance of means of access to and egress from it that are safe and without such risks;

(e) the provision and maintenance of a working environment for his employees that is, so far as is reasonably practicable, safe, without risks to health, and adequate as regards facilities and arrangements for their welfare at work.

(3) Except in such cases as may be prescribed, it shall be the duty of every employer to prepare and as often as may be appropriate revise a written statement of his general policy with respect to the health and safety at work of his employees and the organisation and arrangements for the time being in force for carrying out that policy, and to bring the statement and any revision of it to the notice of all his employees.

(4) Regulations made by the Secretary of State may provide for the appointment in prescribed cases by recognised trade unions (within the meaning of the regulations) of safety representatives from amongst the employees, and those representatives shall represent the employees in consultations with the employers under subsection (6) below and shall have such other functions as may be prescribed.

(5) [Note: this subsection is repealed by the Employment Protection Act 1975]

(6) It shall be the duty of every employer to consult any such representatives with a view to the making and maintenance of arrangements which will enable him and his employees to co-operate effectively in promoting and developing measures to ensure the health and safety at work of the employees, and in checking the effectiveness of such measures.

(7) In such cases as may be prescribed, it shall be the duty of every employer, if requested to do so by the safety representatives mentioned in subsection (4) above, to establish, in accordance with regulations made by the Secretary of State, a safety committee having the function of keeping under review the measures taken to ensure the health and safety at work of his employees and such other functions as may be prescribed.

NOTES

Modification

Sub-ss (1)–(3) modified, in relation to an activity involving genetic modification, by the Genetically Modified Organisms (Contained Use) Regulations 2000

Health and Safety at Work Act 1974 (Section 2 – general duties)

VOCABULARY

A Understanding expressions

Choose the best explanation for each word or phrase from Section 2 of the Act.

1 '... *so far as is reasonably practicable* ...' (Section 2(1))
   a) to the extent that it is reasonably useful
   b) to the extent that it is reasonably capable of being done
2 '*Without prejudice to the generality of* an employer's duty ... (Section 2(2))
   a) Without being generally biased towards ...
   b) Without affecting the general nature of ...
3 '... under *the preceding subsection* ...' (Section 2(2))
   a) the subsection before
   b) the subsection after
4 '... maintenance of *means of access to and egress from* it ...' (Section 2(2)d)
   a) methods of agreeing and disagreeing with
   b) ways into and out of
5 'Except in *such cases as may be prescribed*, ...' (Section 2(3))
   a) those cases which may be specified
   b) those cases which may be excepted
6 '... to *bring* the statement and any revision of it *to the notice of* ...' (Section 2(3))
   a) present as a written notice
   b) bring to the attention of
7 '... this subsection is *repealed* by ...' (Section 2(5))
   a) cancelled
   b) repeated
8 '... in promoting and developing *measures* ...' (Section 2(6))
   a) measurements
   b) methods

B Prepositions

Complete these phrases from the Act using the correct prepositions.

1 .... connection ....
2 .... respect ....
3 .... accordance ....

C Vocabulary development

1 **Choose the correct meaning for *such* in each of these phrases.**

   1 '... *such* information, instruction, ... *as* is necessary ...' (Section 2(2)c)
      a) the information, instruction, etc. of the kind already described
      b) information, instruction, of the kind that is needed
   2 '... without *such* risks ...' (Section 2(2)d)
      a) without risks of the kind already described
      b) without risks of any kind

2 **Underline where the two forms of *such* shown in Exercise 1 are used in Sections 2(6) and 2(7).**

3 **Explain exactly which representatives and which measures are being referred to in Section 2(6).**

4 **Look at Sections 2(4) and 2(6) of the Act. Complete these explanations with *shall*, *will* or *may*.**

1 .... means it refers to the future.
2 .... means it is authorised.
3 .... means it is an obligation.

D Sentence completion

Use words and phrases from Exercises B and C to complete these sentences. The sentences are adapted from the Consumer Protection Act 1987, which regulates liability for injury and damage caused by defective products.

1 This part .... [a] have effect for the purpose of making .... [b] provision .... [c] is necessary in order to comply with the product liability Directive.
2 Subject to the following provisions, where any damage is caused wholly or partly by a defect in a product, every person to whom subsection (2) below applies .... be liable for the damage.
3 Safety regulations may contain provision .... [a] the conditions that .... [b] be attached to any approval given under the regulations.
4 In determining who has suffered any loss of or damage to property and when any .... loss or damage occurred ...
5 The Secretary of State .... serve on any person a notice prohibiting that person from supplying any goods described in the notice.
6 Any goods shall be destroyed .... [a] such directions .... [b] the court may give.

OVER TO YOU

1 Section 2(2)b refers to *arrangements for ensuring [...] safety and absence of risks to health in connection with the use, handling, storage and transport of articles and substances.* In practical terms, what could these arrangements include?

2 Look at the following extract. How would you go about getting the 'safety' message across to employers in an effective way? Discuss your ideas and draw up a list of six or seven key steps.

The British Safety Council (BSC) operates in more than 50 countries and has more than 8,000 company members. The council recently asked 1,000 employees and 250 business leaders about their attitudes and practices in regard to the environment and health and safety at work.

It found 62 per cent of employees 'had little or no safety training', while '49 per cent of bosses don't have or can't be bothered to put a safety management system in place'. Some 51 per cent of employers 'had not even bothered to offer training despite the fact that they could be saving billions of pounds in payouts and costs', the BSC said.

3 The Health and Safety at Work Act featured in this unit concerns the workplace. What about employees who spend a lot of time driving on company business, for example truck drivers or salespeople? What steps should employers take to ensure their safety is properly monitored? Prepare a mini 'health and safety policy', a list of basic rules that company drivers should follow. You can aim this at a specific group of drivers (e.g. salespeople) or you can produce a general policy.

UNIT 13

Contract law

This unit looks at two extracts from a book on the English law of contract.

BEFORE YOU READ

Discuss these questions.

1 What do you need to have a legally binding contract?

2 In English law, a contract does not have to be in writing – it can be in spoken form. This is known as an *oral contract*. Is an oral contract enforceable in your country? What are the practical disadvantages of an oral agreement?

3 With the worldwide increase in Internet commerce, more and more contracts are being made over the Internet. How can these contracts be enforced, as there is nothing in writing between the buyer and the seller?

> **Legal note**
> *Contract* and *agreement* are generally interchangeable.

READING 1

A Understanding the main points

Read the extract on the opposite page and answer this question.

Although oral agreements can exist in English law, how does the case of *Hadley v Kemp* show they are not always ideal?

B Understanding details

Read the extract again and answer these questions.

1 What do most people talk about when asked what a contract is?

2 Give examples of when we can make contracts which are not in writing, perhaps not even put into spoken words.

3 *Royalties* are payments made for the sale of songs and other copyright material. What did the other members of Spandau Ballet want from songwriter and group member Gary Kemp?

VOCABULARY 1

A Legal terminology

Complete these phrases from the extract which correspond to the meanings given.

1 ... an agreement must do particular things specified by the law ...

... an agreement must *s*........ certain *r*........ (paragraph A)

The formalities of a contract

A Ask most people to describe a contract, and they will talk about a piece of paper – the documents you sign when you start a job, buy a house or hire a car, for example. While it is certainly true that these documents are often contracts, in law the term has a wider meaning, covering any legally binding agreement, written or unwritten. In order to be legally binding, an agreement must satisfy certain requirements; but with a few exceptions, being in writing is not one of those requirements. We make contracts when we buy goods at the supermarket, when we get on a bus or a train, and when we put money into a machine to buy chocolate or drinks – all without a word being written down, or sometimes even spoken.

B So, the general rule of contract law is that an agreement does not have to take a specific written form in order to be deemed a binding contract. Often the contract will be simply oral. As it can be difficult to prove later what was agreed orally, there are practical advantages of putting a contract in writing, despite there being no legal requirements to do so. In *Hadley v Kemp* (1999), Gary Kemp was the songwriter in the pop group Spandau Ballet. He was sued by other members of the group for royalties received for the group's music. The basis of their claim was that there had been an oral agreement to share these royalties. They were unable to prove the existence of any oral agreement and so their action failed.

C Of course, most complex transactions are made in writing, and this clearly helps the parties prove their case if there is any disagreement, but usually lack of written formalities will not prevent a court from finding a contract.

2 ... an agreement does not have to be written in any special way ...
... an agreement does not have to t........ a specific w........ f........ (paragraph B)

3 ... in order to be treated as a contract that all parties are committed to.
... in order to be d........ a b........ c......... (paragraph B)

4 ... there are advantages of making a written contract
... there are advantages of p........ a contract i........ w........ (paragraph B)

5 ... no things that the law says are necessary to do so.
... no l........ r........ to do so. (paragraph B)

6 A civil action was started against him ...
He was s......... ... (paragraph B)

7 ... a contract which is not in writing ...
... there had been an o........ a........ to ... (paragraph B)

8 ... so their court case was not successful.
... so their a........ f......... (paragraph B)

9 ... missing formal written details ...
... usually l........ of written f........ will not ... (paragraph C)

10 ... will not prevent a court from deciding there is a contract.
... will not prevent a court from f........ a contract. (paragraph C)

READING 2

A Understanding the main points

Read the extract on the opposite page and answer this question.

Why exactly did the EU introduce legislation that governs the making of contracts over the Internet?

B Understanding details

Read the extract again and answer these questions.

1 What sort of commercial contracts are being made over the Internet?
2 What should service providers do *in general* to make sure buyers can give their 'full and informed consent' before they enter into a contract?
3 What are the three *specific* requirements mentioned under the Electronic Commerce Regulations?
4 What is the effect of Article 9 of the European Electronic Commerce Directive?

VOCABULARY 2

A Understanding expressions

1 **Choose the best option to answer each question.**

1 What does a state or government do when it wants to bring in a new law? (paragraph A)
a) It *declares* a law.
b) It *announces* a law.
c) It *passes* a law.

2 How do lawyers sometimes refer to the final acceptance and signing of a contract? (paragraph B)
a) the termination of a contract
b) the conclusion of a contract
c) the agreement of a contract

2 **Choose the best option to complete each statement.**

1 When a new law first begins to operate, it is brought into ... (paragraph A)
a) ... life. b) ... force. c) ... action.

2 If a business does not obey new regulations, it does not ... (paragraph A)
a) ... comply with them. b) ... apply to them. c) ... contend with them.

B Word families

Complete the chart.

verb	noun
to require	........[1]
to claim	........[2]
........[3]	proof
to agree	........[4]
to conclude	........[5]
........[6]	compliance

Contracts made over the Internet and by e-mail

A Increasingly, contracts are being made over the Internet. In particular, the Internet is being used to order goods and services from suppliers. The European Union is keen to promote the development of a European Internet industry. It has therefore passed the European Electronic Commerce Directive. The Directive lays down some specific formalities that will need to be followed in order to make binding contracts over the Internet. Thus, Article 10 imposes a general requirement on service providers to give a clear account, prior to the conclusion of the contract, of the steps which must be followed to complete the contract online, to ensure 'full and informed consent'. This part of the Directive had been brought into force by the Electronic Commerce (EC Directive) Regulations 2002. Under these Regulations, companies must provide receipts for orders placed electronically without delay, allow customers to change an order easily before buying and provide information such as business e-mail addresses. Businesses which do not comply with the regulations face having to pay statutory damages to customers or receiving a 'stop now' order which will force them to change their procedures.

B Article 9 of the Directive requires Member States to ensure that their legal systems allow contracts to be concluded by electronic means. There must be nothing in the law of the Member States to prevent or affect the validity of a contract concluded electronically just because it was so concluded.

C Sentence completion

Use words from Exercise B in the correct form to complete these sentences.

1 The new consumer safety laws will impose tough new .... on manufacturers.

2 If we do not .... with the new regulations, we could be fined heavily.

3 Prior to the .... of a contract on the Internet, the supplier must ensure that the buyer has given 'full and informed consent'.

4 These are our terms of business, which you accepted. We both signed. So it's a legally binding ....!

5 The company refuses to pay any compensation, so the suppliers are going to make a .... for damages.

6 Without a receipt, it's very difficult to .... where you bought that camera and how much you paid.

D Legal terminology

Complete these phrases from the extract above which correspond to the meanings given.

1 The Directive specifies some formalities ...

The Directive *l*........ *d*........ some formalities (paragraph A)

2 Service providers are required by Article 10 to ...

Article 10 *i*........ a general requirement *o*........ service providers to ... (paragraph A)

OVER TO YOU

1 In a common law system, many of the details agreed between two parties must be expressly included in the contract they sign. In a civil law system, key provisions are already contained in a civil code, and do not have to be written into each contract. Discuss what the advantages and disadvantages of these two systems are, particularly in a business context.

2 Contracts are a key part of any business – for hiring staff, renting an office, servicing equipment. Prepare a five-minute presentation highlighting the typical areas where contracts are necessary in a business you are familiar with.

UNIT 14 Terms and conditions: the language of contracts

This unit looks at an extract from an international distribution agreement: a distributor contracts with a manufacturer to promote, sell and distribute the manufacturer's products in a specific country. The contract terms form the basis of their agreement together.

BEFORE YOU READ

Discuss these questions.

1 If you agreed to be a distributor in your country for, say, a brand of sports shoes and clothes, manufactured abroad, what terms and conditions would you expect to discuss before signing a contract?

2 What kind of language can you expect to find in commercial contracts? Is it the same as everyday, spoken language, or can it often contain special expressions found only in contracts? Give some examples of typical 'contract' words and phrases.

> **Legal note**
> Broadly speaking, *terms* and *conditions* have the same meaning.

READING

A Understanding the main points

Read the extract from a distribution agreement on the opposite page and answer these questions.

1 What are the seven key areas of agreement this extract covers? What is a quick way of finding out information like this?

2 Words starting with a capital letter indicate they are specifically defined somewhere in the contract, usually in the Definitions Clause (not shown in this extract). Which such words can you identify in Clause 1?

B Understanding details

Read the extract again and say whether these statements are true (T) or false (F). Correct the false ones.

1 Both manufacturer and distributor must state what their official registered business address is.

2 The country or region where the distributor has rights to sell the manufacturer's products is referred to as *the Territory*.

3 The heading to Clause 2, *Term*, has the same meaning as in *terms and conditions*.

4 Rights for distribution of the products in the agreed territory can also be given to other distributors.

5 The distributor must pay for the products to be delivered from the manufacturer to the distributor's shipping agent.

DISTRIBUTION AGREEMENT

This Agreement is made on [*date*] by and between [*Company A*] (the Manufacturer), a company incorporated in [*country*] and having its registered office at [*address*], and [*Company B*] (the Distributor), having its registered office at [*address*].

The parties hereto agree as follows:

1 APPOINTMENT AS DISTRIBUTOR

The Manufacturer appoints the Distributor as its exclusive distributor for [*product range*] (the Products), more specifically described in the Schedule for the Term of this Agreement and all renewals thereof, and grants to the Distributor the right to perform all those services in [*country or region*] (the Territory) with respect to the Products as are normally performed by a manufacturer's stockist, distributor and exclusive sales representative.

2 TERM

This Agreement shall commence on [*date*] and shall be for THREE (3) years (the Initial Term). Thereafter, the Agreement shall be renewed annually and automatically, unless written notice of termination is provided by either party at least SIX (6) months prior to the end of the then current contract year.

3 DISTRIBUTION RIGHTS AND DUTIES

a) The Distributor shall have exclusive distribution in the Territory for the Products. The Manufacturer shall refer all orders from the Territory to the Distributor and such orders shall be fulfilled by the Distributor.

b) The Distributor shall provide warehousing services for all the Products, and shall promote their sale, process orders, collect payment and ship to customers.

4 SHIPMENT OF PRODUCTS

a) Risk of loss of or damage to any consignment of the Products shall pass to the Distributor from the time the Products are delivered to the Distributor's shipping agent.

b) The Manufacturer shall bear the cost of delivery of the Products to the Distributor's shipping agent. Upon receipt of the Products, the Distributor shall arrange and bear the cost (including insurance cost) for the Products to be unloaded, stored and shipped to the Distributor's own warehouse.

c) The Manufacturer shall ensure that the packing of the Products meets industry standards or such other specifications as may be agreed in writing by the parties and that the Products arrive in good condition at the Distributor's shipping agent. In the event of any defective Products being received, the Manufacturer is obliged to accept their return for replacement or repayment at the invoiced price.

5 ADVERTISING, PROMOTION AND PRODUCT INFORMATION

a) The Distributor shall include each Product distributed by it in accordance with this Agreement in all its appropriate catalogues, brochures, advertisements and exhibitions for which the Distributor shall deem such Products appropriate.

b) The Distributor shall also at its sole discretion use its own mailing lists to promote the Products.

6 PAYMENT

Products supplied by the Manufacturer shall be handled under the following terms:

a) The Distributor agrees to purchase its stock from the Manufacturer at x% discount off the Manufacturer's domestic list price.

b) The Manufacturer shall invoice the Distributor in US dollars on 180 days' credit terms and all payment shall be made by the Distributor in US dollars.

7 RETURNS

The Manufacturer agrees at its sole discretion to accept returns of up to 10% of unsold Products based on the annual turnover of the Distributor with the Manufacturer. Any unsold Products must be in saleable condition to be accepted by the Manufacturer. The Distributor has to bear all the related expenses incurred in returning the Products to the Manufacturer's warehouse.

6 If the manufacturer delivers faulty products, then the manufacturer must replace them or repay the price stated on the invoice.

7 The manufacturer will tell the distributor where to advertise and promote the products.

8 The manufacturer must take back any products not sold by the distributor.

VOCABULARY

A Legal terminology

Find words or phrases in the distribution agreement which fit these meanings.

1 legally established or set up in (agreement introduction)
2 only (Clause 1)
3 a part of the contract where specific details and technical specifications are listed, to avoid writing such details in the main part of the contract (Clause 1)
4 the first period of the agreement (Clause 2)
5 information that one party wishes to end the contract (Clause 2)
6 carried out, completed (e.g. an order, an obligation) (Clause 3a)
7 be responsible for paying for something (Clause 4b)
8 satisfies (a standard, a requirement) (Clause 4c)
9 must (Clause 4c)
10 consider (e.g. to be appropriate) (Clause 5a)
11 the exclusive right to decide (Clause 5b)
12 resulting from (in relation to costs/expenses) (Clause 7)

B Adverbs and prepositions

Contracts written in a formal style contain adverbs such as *hereto*, *hereby*, *therein* and *thereafter*. As a general rule, *here* means 'this document/place/time' – the one we are referring to – and *there* means 'that document/place/time' – a different one.

1 **Find three adverbs in the early part of the distribution agreement to complete the second phrase in each pair.**

   1 the parties *to this* Agreement
     the parties ....
   2 all renewals *of that* Term
     all renewals ....
   3 *after that* time (i.e. after the Initial Term)
     ....

2 **Use the adverbs in the box to complete the second phrase in each pair. There are some adverbs that you will not need.**

hereby	hereto	hereunder	herewith	therefor	therein	thereof

   1 the Schedule attached to this Agreement
     the Schedule attached ....
   2 the technical specifications referred to in that Schedule
     the technical specifications referred to ....
   3 it is agreed by this document
     it is .... agreed
   4 ... the services and the payment for those services
     ... the services and the payment ....

3 **Use the prepositions in the box to complete the sentences from the agreement. Some are used more than once.**

at between by in of on to upon with

1 This Agreement is made ....[a] [*date*] ....[b] and ....[c] Company A and Company B.
2 The Manufacturer grants ....[a] the Distributor the right to perform services ....[b] respect ....[c] the Products as are normally performed ....[d] a distributor.
3 ... unless notice ....[a] termination is provided ....[b] either party ....[c] least six months prior ....[d] the end of the then current year.
4 Risk ....[a] loss ....[b] or damage ....[c] the Products shall pass ....[d] the Distributor ...
5 The Manufacturer shall bear the cost ....[a] delivery ....[b] the Products ....[c] the Distributor's shipping agent. ....[d] receipt ....[e] the Products, the Distributor shall arrange ...
6 ....[a] the event ....[b] any defective Products being received, ...
7 ... each Product distributed ....[a] accordance ....[b] this Agreement.

ILEC C Vocabulary development

Choose the best word to fill the gap from the choices A–D beside the additional extract from the distribution agreement.

8 RESOLUTION OF DISPUTE
This Agreement is made ....[1] to the laws of [*country*]. In the ....[2] of any ....[3] between the ....[4] which cannot be agreed by negotiation, each party shall have the ....[5] to appoint a representative who will then attempt to negotiate on their ....[6], in ....[7] with the regulated ....[8] procedures in [*country*].

	A	B	C	D
1	following	allowing	subject	schedule
2	effort	cases	chance	event
3	deal	dispute	regulation	notice
4	persons	clauses	parties	products
5	right	costs	retention	review
6	breach	case	behalf	contract
7	acquaintance	acceptance	accordance	alteration
8	argument	arbitration	priority	termination

OVER TO YOU

1 You own a studio room that you wish to rent to a student for at least 12 months. The studio is in good condition, it is furnished, and you have provided kitchen equipment and a television. Discuss with a colleague the key points you think the rental contract should include.
2 Find an example of a commercial contract (for instance, bank account or credit-card terms and conditions, a mobile phone contract, car-insurance agreement, etc.). Make notes so that you can summarise the main contents of the contract to a colleague.

UNIT **15**

A case law report

This unit focuses on case law. In common law systems, decisions made by judges when hearing a case establish how the law stands on certain points. Once a precedent is set (i.e. the legal principle has been established), it remains valid law unless changed by a later decision or by legislation.

BEFORE YOU READ

Discuss these questions.

1 Judges are able to make entirely new decisions in court if, for example, they consider that today's circumstances are very different from those applying when the legal precedent was originally established (which might have been many years earlier). What are the advantages of this approach? And are there disadvantages?

2 Think carefully about the circumstances of the case reported here before you read the report: Company A agreed to fit special breakdown equipment to a truck for Company B, and B would then sell the vehicle on to someone else. A fault was discovered in the special equipment that A fitted, but only six months after delivery, when B tried to sell the vehicle on. Do you think B was obliged to accept the truck? What factors do you think the court would have considered?

READING

A Understanding law reports

Read the case report on the opposite page and choose the best option to complete each statement.

1 The background is ...

a) presented in a colourful, descriptive way.
b) stated in a plain, factual manner.

2 Case reports contain ...

a) a lot of specific legal language.
b) mostly language that a non-lawyer could easily understand.

3 The word *Held* (line 21) introduces ...

a) a summary of the arguments presented by the claimant and the defendant.
b) the court's decision, together with an explanation of how the law applies to the situation in question.

B Understanding details

Read the report again and answer these questions.

1 This case concerns a dispute about a contract, but exactly what kind of contract?

2 An HGV is a heavy goods vehicle – a truck, a lorry of some kind. How are HGVs relevant to the agreement between the two companies?

Truk (UK) Ltd v Tokmakidis GmbH[1]

[2000] 1 Lloyd's Rep 543, [2000] 2 All ER (Comm) 594[2]

The claimants, an English company, contracted to supply and fit towing and lifting equipment to a chassis supplied by the defendants, a German company. This was a sale of goods. The essence of the contract was the delivery and sale of the lifting and towing equipment, which would allow broken-down HGV vehicles to be recovered. The claimants delivered the vehicle on 14 June 1996. However, the contract was breached in that the vehicle did not comply with certain guidelines specified in the contract. The defendants had bought the goods for resale. The contract envisaged that the resale of the vehicle might take more than six months, in that it provided that the price should be paid six months after delivery or on resale, whichever was sooner. The defendants had not intimated that they were rejecting until they discovered, in December 1996, that the vehicle did not comply with the contract specifications. (A potential buyer had pointed this out.) The parties then entered into negotiations which lasted until July 1997, when the defendants rejected the goods and refused to accept redelivery of a repaired vehicle.

Held. A reasonable time in which to intimate rejection had not passed. When goods are sold for resale, defects in the goods are often only discovered when the sub-buyer examines the goods. Therefore, a reasonable time in which to intimate rejection of the goods would usually be the time which it would be expected would be needed to resell the goods plus an additional period in which the sub-purchaser might inspect them and try them out. (If the vehicle had not been for resale, a month or two might have been a reasonable time on these facts, although discussions about remedying defects might have extended this period.) In July 1997, the defendants were still entitled to reject because they had done nothing to affirm the contract. Nor were they deemed to have accepted the goods by failing to reject them within a reasonable time. They had reserved their position while they were discovering what was wrong and negotiating, and they were allowed a reasonable time for that.

Legal notes

1 When talking about a case (here, *Truk (UK) Ltd v Tokmakidis GmbH*), lawyers often say *and* instead of *v* or *versus*. The first name is the claimant, the second is the defendant.

2 This report comes from a textbook on business law, but the original source is in Volume 1 of Lloyd's Reports, year 2000, at page 543, or Volume 2 of All England Reports at page 594. Official reports name the judges, the barristers representing the claimant and defendant, the instructing solicitors and the person who wrote the report.

3 When was it agreed that payment should be made?
4 Who discovered that there was a problem with the vehicle?
5 How many months after delivery did the German company reject the truck with the faulty towing equipment?
6 In the court's decision, what is regarded as a 'reasonable time' for rejecting goods sold for resale?
7 What would that 'reasonable time' be for goods not sold for resale, if the circumstances were similar to this case?
8 Was the court's decision in favour of the claimants or the defendants?

VOCABULARY

A Legal terminology

1 **Find words or phrases in the report which fit these meanings.**

1 the two parties opposing one another in a civil claim
c........; d........
2 agreed to do something by means of a contract
c........
3 the central purpose of a contract (in contract law)
the e........ of the contract
4 broken (a contract)
b........
5 obey (e.g. regulations, laws, etc.)
c........ ....
6 not accepting
r........
7 the people or companies who enter into a contract
the p........
8 faults in a product
d........

2 **Letters from words and phrases used in the law report have been jumbled. Form the correct words using the definitions.**

1	an area of contract law relating to items offered for sale	LEAS FO OSDOG
2	the process of transferring a sold item to a buyer	LYVERIED
3	instructions on how things should be done	DENSELUIGI
4	Details (often technical) in a contract of what is to be supplied	STIPIFANISOCCE
5	Payment six months after receipt, or on sale, ... is sooner.	HIVECHEWR
6	the original buyer sells on to this person	BUS-SHARPCURE

B Synonyms

Match the legal expressions (1–7) with their 'everyday English' equivalents (a–g).

1 The contract envisaged that ...
2 They intimated rejection ...
3 The parties entered into negotiations ...
4 The defects have been remedied ...
5 The purchaser was deemed to have accepted the goods.
6 They were entitled to reject...
7 They had reserved their position

a) They have put all the faults right ...
b) They had not decided yet
c) They said that they wouldn't accept ...
d) They had the right to reject ...
e) As far as the law is concerned, they had accepted the goods
f) In the contract, it was expected that ...
g) The two companies started to negotiate ...

C Latin words and phrases

Latin expressions are used widely in the legal profession, particularly in court cases. Here are some that are relatively common. You should note that pronunciation differs from country to country – there is no 'correct' version.

ab initio	from the beginning	ex gratia	as a favour, not a right
ad hoc	for a specific situation	inter alia	among other things
affidavit	a sworn statement	per se	on its own
bona fide	in good faith	subpoena	an order to appear in court
caveat emptor	buyer, take care	ultra vires	beyond a limit of authority

Use the words and phrases in the language box to complete these sentences.

1 The contract was void .... It was invalid right from the start.

2 To tell a lie is not illegal .... But when someone is misled into buying something from you, that can be a different matter.

3 The court issued a ...., so the witness had no choice but to appear in court.

4 The sale description was fine. Completely .... The buyer should've checked things more carefully before he bought. It's a basic rule of buying privately – ....!

5 The director was acting .... when he signed that cheque for €500,000, so the company may not be liable to pay it.

6 She was a member of an .... committee, set up solely to consider current staffing problems.

7 The evidence from one witness was not allowed, as the lawyers had failed to provide an ....

8 To maintain good customer relations, the manufacturers made an .... payment of $150, but they did not admit liability.

9 The accused claimed, ..., that he was a famous sports personality. He deceived people with several different false claims.

OVER TO YOU

1 You are advising a friend who has bought an expensive communication device from a local shop. The camera doesn't work properly, the battery runs down very quickly, the downloads are very slow, and it looks like the box had already been opened before the salesman took it from the shelf. Really, the product doesn't do what the salesman told your friend it would do.

Write a letter of complaint to the shop manager. This need not be a lawyer's letter about misselling and broken contracts, but a business-like letter, setting out the facts clearly, and stating what action you want the shop to take.

2 Work in pairs. You have read the case of *Truk (UK) Ltd v Tokmakidis GmbH*. A colleague of yours wants to know all about it – what happened, and what the court decided. Your colleague is not a legal specialist, so may not understand technical legal words. Make notes so you can tell the whole story in your own words, without having to refer back to the report. Ask your colleague to summarise what you have said.

3 Find a different case report and give a short spoken summary of it. Explain in your own words what the case is about, what the area of law is, who the parties are, what the background is and what the court decided.

UNIT 16 How tax laws can create business

This unit looks at how some countries – known as *tax havens* – offer favourable tax laws, which attract companies from around the world.

BEFORE YOU READ

Discuss these questions.

1 International business leaders can earn vast sums of money. What steps can they take to keep as much of their wealth as possible from being paid away in tax?

2 What are the attractions of a country that has strict banking secrecy laws? Are there any financial activities that no bank should keep confidential?

3 Tax evasion is illegal, but tax avoidance is legal. How do large organisations set up tax-avoidance schemes? Is this something the ordinary individual can also do for him- or herself?

READING

A Understanding the main points

Read the article on the opposite page and answer these questions.

1 Are Singapore's banking laws attractive because they are very strict, or because they are quite open and flexible? And are the tax laws there very tough, or quite favourable?

2 Why did certain Swiss banks move some of their major operations to Singapore?

3 Which areas of Singapore's banking and tax laws have the US, the EU and the OECD become involved with?

B Understanding details

Read the article again and say whether these statements are true (T) or false (F). Correct the false ones.

1 The EU Savings Directive helped Singapore because it said non-European bank operations must be moved to Singapore.

2 In Singapore, international tax evasion is not illegal.

3 Singapore taxes are favourable to both individuals and companies.

4 Singapore has an open, flexible approach to exchanging banking information with other countries.

5 Singapore has banking operations in the US.

6 Singapore banks are freely offering more local bank-account information to foreign governments.

7 Singapore is not willing to comply with the EU Savings Directive.

8 If Singapore accepts the OECD rules, this will attract more private banks to set up business there.

Singapore tax laws attract wealth-management businesses

by Jack Burton

A Officials hate Singapore being described as a tax haven. They prefer to say it is a low-tax jurisdiction.

B Singapore's rise as a wealth-management centre for those outside Asia got a boost in 2005 with the adoption of the European Union Savings Directive, under which banks in tax sanctuaries such as Switzerland must impose withholding taxes on accounts held by EU citizens if the names of the account holders are not revealed. In response, Credit Suisse and UBS established their biggest private-banking operations outside Switzerland in Singapore, and were followed by smaller European private banks.

C What attracted them to Singapore was the bank secrecy laws, which are among the world's strictest. In addition, the country has no law against international tax evasion. 'Under current law, Singapore will not assist in tax-evasion cases in foreign jurisdictions,' says Edmund Leow, a tax lawyer in Singapore.

D Singapore does not tax the global income of those holding local bank accounts. Residents are subject to a maximum tax rate of 20 per cent on local salary income, and investment income is tax-free. The corporate tax rate will be cut by 1 percentage point to 17 per cent this year, making it among the lowest in the world.

E Singapore's bank secrecy laws are based on British common law, inherited from its former colonial rulers. Although it has signed double-taxation treaties with 60 countries, 'Singapore has been much more restrictive than the UK in the exchange of information under these treaties', says Leow.

F An important exception is its qualified intermediary agreement with the US, which requires all foreign banks that operate in the US to disclose overseas bank accounts held by US citizens. Singapore also has laws banning the laundering of money from internationally recognised illegal activities, such as drug trafficking and financial fraud, or funds looted from national treasuries by foreign leaders or their families. 'We do not stand for the abuse of our laws to shelter criminals,' Lim Hwee Hua, a senior finance ministry official, told parliament recently. But Singapore is under growing pressure from foreign governments to disclose more information about local bank accounts to counter tax evasion.

G One important test of the city-state's determination to maintain bank secrecy has been a demand by the EU that Singapore – along with Hong Kong – accept the EU Savings Directive. So far, Singapore has refused to do so, and the dispute has blocked the signing of an EU–Singapore partnership agreement to promote closer co-operation.

H In addition, Singapore could attract the attention of the administration in the US, which has promised to take strong action against countries that it sees as tax havens.

I Singapore appears to be relaxing its position somewhat. The government is considering adopting standards set by the Organisation for Economic Co-operation and Development for transparency and effective exchange of tax information. Under the OECD rules, Singapore would have to assist with information requests on specific tax-evasion cases from its tax treaty partners.

J How far Singapore is willing to go to disclose information under the OECD rules will be important for the future of its private banking industry, which is a key component of the financial services sector. An aggressive enforcement of the rules would probably drive away some private banks.

FT

VOCABULARY

A Word search

Find words and phrases in the article which fit these meanings.

1. three expressions for a place where tax laws are favourable (paragraphs A and B)
2. two verbs meaning 'to make public', 'to not keep hidden' (paragraphs B and F)
3. legislation which is effective at present (paragraph C)
4. the legal territories of other countries (paragraph C)
5. passed down, often through families (but here from one ruling power to another) (paragraph E)
6. a person or organisation that is a link between other separate parties, in finance or in negotiations, for example (paragraph F)
7. prohibiting, forbidding (paragraph F)
8. processing illegally gained profits so the money cannot be traced (paragraph F)
9. things people do which are against the law (paragraph F)
10. illegally getting money from a company or individual (paragraph F)

B Understanding expressions

Choose the best explanation for each phrase from the article.

1 '... must *impose withholding taxes on accounts* ...' (lines 10–11)
   a) require the deduction of tax directly from accounts
   b) pay a special tax on accounts

2 '... or *funds looted from national treasuries* by ...' (lines 53–54)
   a) profits earned from national museums
   b) money stolen from state finance resources

3 'We do not *stand for the abuse of our laws to shelter criminals* ...' (lines 54–56)
   a) support criminals in our laws
   b) allow people to use our laws to protect criminals

4 '... to *counter tax evasion*.' (lines 61–62)
   a) act against tax evasion
   b) find the total number of tax evasion cases

5 '... the dispute has *blocked* the signing of an [...] agreement ...' (lines 68–71)
   a) led to
   b) prevented

6 'The government is considering *adopting* standards ...' (lines 78–79)
   a) putting into use
   b) changing

7 '... for *transparency* and effective exchange ...' (lines 81–82)
   a) when business practices are carried out openly
   b) when financial transfers can be made easily

C Word partnerships

Complete the sentences below using financial and legal word partnerships formed by combining a word from Box A with a word from Box B. The word *tax* can be used more than once.

A
bank common corporate double-taxation income tax wealth withholding

B
evasion haven law management secrecy tax treaty

1 Rich individuals might like to have a bank account in a ....
2 The business of looking after the funds of people with a lot of personal money is called ....
3 When a bank does not pay 100% of interest earned on a bank account, what it keeps and passes to the state revenue office is known as ....
4 Singapore has strict .... laws, which makes it an attractive place for wealthy individuals to keep money.
5 .... is an illegal practice; avoidance schemes, however, are perfectly legal.
6 Individuals pay .... to the state on their earnings; companies pay .... on profits.
7 England has a ....-........ system, in contrast to the civil codes of many other countries.
8 An agreement between countries to take into account each others tax collection procedures is called a ....-........ ....

D Word families

Complete the chart.

verb	noun
to sign	 1
.... 2	evasion
to avoid	 3
to disclose	 4
.... 5	ban
to demand	 6
to assist	 7
to refuse	 8

OVER TO YOU

1 You work as an adviser to wealthy investors. Give a summary to a potential client of the advantages of Singapore as a tax haven, also explaining its position in relation to the EU, the US and the OECD.
2 Do some research on the Internet or from books or magazines so you can give a brief overview of two other tax havens, paying particular attention to any changes that may have taken place in the past few years.
3 The attitude to paying taxes varies widely in different parts of the world. What do individuals think about the current tax regime in your country? Explain to someone from another country what the general view is about what is good, what could be changed, and whether it is acceptable to avoid paying taxes wherever possible.

UNIT 17

Insider dealing

Insider dealing, or insider trading, is the illegal trading of a company's shares by staff who have confidential company information that would affect the share price.

BEFORE YOU READ

Discuss these questions.

1 What are the practical problems facing any regulatory authority that wants to monitor the complex trading activities of international bankers and financial traders?

2 What kind of punishment is appropriate for insider dealing on a large scale? Is a substantial fine going to be an effective deterrent, or should there always be a prison sentence?

READING

A Understanding the main points

Read the article on the opposite page and answer these questions.

1 What sort of action is being taken by the US government to control insider trading?

2 What kind of job did Mr Plotkin have at Goldman? What kind of jobs present the biggest difficulties in bringing a case for insider dealing?

ILEC B Understanding details

The article has been divided into four sections – A, B, C and D. Read the article again and answer the questions about each section.

Section A

1 Which lines tell us about the two key topic areas of this article – insider dealing by individuals, and by groups of people?

2 Does the writer say Mr Plotkin's case ...

a) has caused the US government to take action on insider dealing, or
b) is an illustration of how the government is already taking action?

Section B

3 What was Mr Gourevitch's opinion about how Mr Plotkin carried out his insider trading scheme?

4 A *seamstress* is a woman who sews clothes for a living. Why did the writer include the information about *a retired Croatian seamstress*?

Section C

5 Why does Mr Gourevitch think it is 'virtually impossible' to make a case against professional traders?

a) Because they are protected from investigations.
b) Because their work is very complex, and they know how to explain it in plausible detail.
c) Because they buy and sell so quickly that nobody can trace the trades they have been involved in.

Insider dealing sentence highlights crackdown

by Ben White

Section A

The sentencing of Eugene Plotkin, former Goldman Sachs analyst, to nearly five years in prison highlights the continuing crackdown by the US government on illicit insider trading.

However, legal analysts said it also acted as a reminder that, while certain colourful schemes such as the one put together by Mr Plotkin were fairly easy for the government to detect, insider trades by sophisticated Wall Street groups such as hedge funds remained much harder to uncover. 'Clearly there is a broad crackdown going on here. The government has brought several of these cases in the last year,' said David Gourevitch, a defence attorney and former prosecutor.

Section B

Mr Gourevitch noted that several of the cases were similar to the one involving Mr Plotkin in that they also involved highly unusual activity by seemingly unsophisticated traders.

Some of the trades involved in Mr Plotkin's case were allegedly made in an account registered to a retired Croatian seamstress.

Section C

Mr Gourevitch said it was much more difficult for the government to discover insider trading among highly sophisticated investors. 'It is virtually impossible to make a case against someone who is a professional trader in hedge funds and the like,' he said. 'Because they are going in and out of so many stocks every day, they are surrounded by market gossip and they usually have huge amounts of information about all the things they are trading, so they can explain why they did what they did.'

Section D

Mr Plotkin, a former fixed-income research associate at Goldman and one-time competitive ballroom dancer, was sentenced to 57 months in prison for his role in a scheme that prosecutors say produced more than $6.7m in illicit gains. Mr Plotkin, who pleaded guilty, allegedly received inside information from several sources, including an analyst at Merrill Lynch and a grand juror in New Jersey who prosecutors said supplied tips about a government investigation into Bristol-Myers Squibb, the drugs company.

Prosecutors said Mr Plotkin also tried to hire strippers to obtain information from investment bankers about pending merger deals.

Other alleged co-conspirators included two employees of a printing plant who the government said stole advance copies of BusinessWeek magazine and provided information from the Inside Wall Street column. Another former Goldman employee, David Pajcin, has pleaded guilty, as have other alleged co-conspirators.

The scheme, planned in a Russian-style health spa, was said by the government to include illegal trades on pending deals, including Adidas's acquisition of Reebok International in 2006.

FT

Section D

6 Why does the writer include the information that Mr Plotkin was a *one-time competitive ballroom dancer* and that the scheme was planned in *a Russian-style health spa*?

7 In order to make his trades, how did Mr Plotkin obtain the necessary information? Give details of all the sources and methods he used.

8 Why does the writer use the words *alleged* and *allegedly* several times in this section?

VOCABULARY

A Word search

Find words or phrases in the article which fit these meanings.

1 a court order to spend time in prison (title)
2 the strict enforcement of rules (usually to stop undesirable activities) (title)
3 illegal (Section A)
4 the opposite of *basic, simple, uncomplicated* (Section A)
5 in the US, a lawyer who represents the accused (Section A)
6 adjective describing a previous occupation (Section A)
7 in the US, a lawyer who represents the prosecution (Section A)
8 indicates a claimed fact that has yet to be proved in court (Section B)
9 stories and rumours, not necessarily true (Section C)
10 admitted in court that he was guilty (Section D)
11 in the US, a member of a special jury which decides whether criminal proceedings should be started (Section D)
12 to recruit (Section D)
13 when two companies join together to form one company (Section D)
14 adjective describing something which has not yet been finalised (Section D)
15 a takeover (Section D)

B Word families

Complete the chart.

verb	noun
........[1]	sentence/sentencing
to remind	........[2]
to prosecute	........[3] (person) ....[4] (activity)
........[5]	retirement
to invest	........[6] (person) ....[7] (activity)
to investigate	........[8] (person) ....[9] (activity)
........[10]	allegation

C Sentence completion

Use the correct form of words from Exercise B to complete these sentences.

1 It was an excellent .... I made a profit of $2,000!
2 The chairman .... last year. He was 65.
3 The case for the .... was very strong. They had a lot of evidence against the accused.

4 The way the company conducted its financial activities .... thoroughly by the police.

5 'Will he remember to phone tomorrow?' 'I think he'll need a ....'

6 We believe a prison .... has more effect than a fine.

7 He had a successful career in court as a ....

8 It is .... that the Financial Director transferred funds to his personal account.

9 All .... have been warned that the company is in difficulties, and they could lose a lot of money.

10 The police .... lasted for four days – they asked office staff various questions relating to the robbery.

ILEC **D**

Text completion

Read this extract about insider dealing and write the best word to fill each gap.

FSA on alert over insider dealing concerns

by Gillian Tett

The Financial Services Authority is closely monitoring the London markets over concerns that the recent turmoil in bank shares ....[1] have encouraged insider dealing.

Executives at the FSA, the UK financial services regulator, think that some investors may be seeking to ....[2] advantage of the recent swings in share prices.

The FSA has consistently defended its record on stopping market abuse, saying that policing insider traders has been particularly difficult ....[3] complex derivative transactions – not easily visible to the market – are often used.

To this end, the FSA is looking at introducing US-style plea bargaining for suspected insider dealers. This could see suspects offered lesser punishments, or even immunity, in ....[4] for co-operating with the FSA.

'For insider dealers, it becomes an economic calculation. If the worst that can happen is a fine, then they won't think twice. But if jail comes into it, a suspect trade becomes a totally ....[5] story,' said one hedge-fund manager at a large City firm.

FT

E

Vocabulary development

Letters from words in the extract in Exercise D have been jumbled. Form the correct words, using the definitions, then find the words in the extract.

1	observing a process closely	GRINNITOOM
2	confusion	MOULRIT
3	an official body	ALUGETORR
4	movements like a pendulum	GWISSN
5	keeping a watch on	CLIPIONG
6	freedom from prosecution	MIYTUMNI

OVER TO YOU

1 Mr Plotkin was given a prison sentence of nearly five years, but it appears many other traders may have carried out illegal deals undetected. Was Mr Plotkin's greatest mistake to get caught? Do you feel his prison sentence was a fair punishment, or was it more of an example, to warn other more sophisticated operators? Discuss your views with a colleague.

2 Insider dealing is, in essence, gaining an unfair advantage by using information that by law you cannot use. What other situations are there where, legally or ethically, you should not use information in this way? Write an essay of around 300 words, giving examples.

UNIT 18 Sharia law and international finance

This unit looks at how non-Muslim countries are adapting their financial regulations so that Islamic finance has access to the many business opportunities on offer.

The article includes important Islamic terms:

sharia	Islamic religious law (applies to many aspects of everyday life, including financial matters)
sharia-compliant	complying with sharia; for example, payment of interest is not sharia-compliant
sukuk	an Islamic financial certificate, similar to a bond
takaful	a type of Islamic insurance

BEFORE YOU READ

Discuss these questions.

1 From a business point of view, what are the advantages of ensuring that your economy is open to investment from around the world?

2 Which laws regulate the financing and taxation of business in your country? How can these laws be amended, for example to bring them up to date?

READING

A Understanding the main points

Read the article on the opposite page and answer these questions.

1 Bearing in mind the severe economic downturn experienced by investments in conventional Western assets in late 2008, why should Islamic finance appear attractive to non-Muslim countries?

2 How have the various countries mentioned been able to adapt their financial frameworks so as to be acceptable to Islamic finance?

B Understanding details

Read the article again and answer these questions.

1 What are the two main principles mentioned that relate to Islamic finance?

2 The Dow Jones Islamic Market index lost 2.74 per cent. Why was this considered to be a 'good' performance?

3 What has created the substantial funds of money in the Middle East?

4 What steps have been taken by the FSA in the UK to open up the market to Islamic finance?

5 What are the different measures France and Germany have taken to attract Islamic finance?

6 What is the significance of Turkey's substantial Muslim population?

7 Which country is seen as a rival to Hong Kong?

Leap of faith

by Farmida Bi and Aziza Atta

A Some non-Muslim countries are now making regulatory changes to ensure that their domestic companies are able to access liquidity in 5 the Middle East.

B A depressed global financial situation will see increasing attention being paid to Islamic financial solutions and a keen interest shown by 10 some countries in promoting Islamic finance. The principles underlying Islamic finance, where capital must be used in a genuine commercial activity and full disclosure is required 15 to avoid uncertainty as to the nature of the contract that the parties are entering into, are likely to be an integral part of any reformation of the conventional system that is sure 20 to follow an economic crisis.

C As the conventional markets collapsed under the stresses of the latter part of 2008, a number of market participants began to 25 comment on the relative health of Islamic institutions, which did not acquire toxic assets in the economic crisis. The Dow Jones Islamic Market (DJIM) indexes performed well, 30 with the DJIM Financials Index losing 2.74 per cent and the Dow Jones Citigroup Sukuk Index losing 0.27 per cent during the turmoil in September, when conventional 35 indexes suffered losses of more than 20 per cent.

D The UK has worked hard to establish London as the international financial centre for Islamic finance 40 through introducing tax and regulatory changes to ensure that Islamic finance has a 'level playing field' with conventional finance. The Financial Services Authority has authorised 45 six wholly Islamic banks, and the UK Government is thinking about issuing a sharia-compliant gilt or bill-like sukuks.

E The success of the UK, together 50 with the large pools of liquidity available in the Middle East generated from record oil prices, have encouraged other non-Muslim countries in Europe and Asia to review their legal 55 systems to ensure that their institutions are able to access sharia-compliant products.

F France
The French government and the 60 French financial markets regulatory authority announced significant tax and regulatory changes aimed at promoting Islamic finance in France. These changes relate to the listing of 65 sukuk, the tax treatment of Islamic finance transactions and the introduction of trusts into French law.

G Germany
The federal state of Saxony-Anhalt 70 issued Europe's first Islamic bond in July 2004, and there is increasing interest in Islamic finance from the private sector; for example, the Munich-based FWU Group won 75 the award for Best Takaful Operator in 2007.

H Italy
The Italian Banking Association and the Union of Arab Banks entered 80 into a memorandum of understanding in September 2007 to promote Islamic finance in Italy, including the establishment of Islamic banks in the country.

I Turkey
Although Turkey has a Muslim population of 72 million, it is run as a secular state. Its Islamic finance sector is tiny, accounting for less 90 than 5 per cent of deposits, and the issue of whether Islamic finance should be allowed to grow is highly political. Turkey, however, has the greatest potential for expansion of 95 Islamic finance in Europe.

J Japan
The Japanese government is keen to develop Islamic finance; there has been talk of a quasi-sovereign 100 sukuk issue by the Japan Bank for International Co-operation. In December 2007, the Japanese Financial Services Agency proposed that Japanese banking regulations 105 should be amended to allow subsidiaries of banks to offer Islamic finance products. Daiwa Asset Management launched the Sharia Japan 100 Index, which includes 110 Japan's top 100 sharia-compliant companies.

K Hong Kong
The Hong Kong Monetary Authority has formed a working group to 115 establish the necessary laws, tax systems and other regulations to put Islamic finance on an equal basis with its conventional counterpart. Hong Kong is seeking to position 120 itself as the intermediary for structuring and marketing Islamic finance products to meet the needs of businesses in mainland China and Middle Eastern invest- 125 ors, although it is facing competition from Singapore.

from *The Lawyer*

VOCABULARY

A Word search

Find words or phrases in the article which fit these meanings.

1 cash, readily available money (paragraph A)
2 adjective describing assets which have been 'infected' and can destroy investments (paragraph C)
3 had/experienced (losses) (paragraph C)
4 a fair situation which doesn't favour any parties involved (paragraph D)
5 a British government security (paragraph D)
6 placing on the stock exchange (paragraph F)
7 non-state-owned businesses (paragraph G)
8 the opposite of *parent companies* (paragraph J)
9 put a new product or service on the market (paragraph J)
10 a person or organisation acting as a link for other separate parties (paragraph K)

B Legal terminology

1 **Find words or phrases in the article which fit these meanings.**

1 alterations made to legal regulations (paragraph A)
2 to look again at an existing law or legal process (paragraph E)
3 arrangements where someone is given the power to look after money on behalf of someone else (paragraph F)
4 a document setting out how parties intend to proceed. It is usually to record wishes, rather than being a legally enforceable agreement. (paragraph H)
5 prefix used to indicate something is like something else, is almost something else (paragraph J)
6 changed, altered (used especially with laws and regulations) (paragraph J)

2 **Read this explanation of a trust, then answer the questions.**

A trust is a fiduciary arrangement in which the trustee – a company or an individual – is given the power to deal with money – the trust fund – on behalf of a beneficiary or beneficiaries. Banks are frequently trustees; the trust gives them the power to invest money from the trust fund and pay interest to beneficiaries. There may be a living trust, where the settlor – the person who creates the trust – is alive. Or there can be a testamentary trust, where the settlor dies, and his or her will is the trust instrument – the trust deed – which specifies how the trustees should deal with the trust fund on behalf of the beneficiaries. Trustees have a duty to invest with care, always keeping the best interests of the beneficiaries in mind. Trustees can also be authorised to deal with property, such as land and buildings.

1 Which three parties are needed for a trust?
2 Which adjective means *based on trust*?
3 What is the difference between a living trust and a testamentary trust?
4 What document passes on your property when you die?
5 What is the name of the document that creates a trust?
6 Can trustees invest money from the trust fund any way they like?

C Vocabulary development

The article is about regulatory *changes* in non-Muslim countries. Find two further words used in the article (paragraphs B and J) that relate to change.

D Word families

Complete the chart.

verb	noun
to change	........[1]
........[2]	reformation
to amend	........[3]
to vary	........[4]
........[5]	modification
to alter	........[6]

E Prepositions

Complete these sentences using the correct prepositions, then check your answers in the article.

1 These changes relate ....[a] the listing ....[b] sukuk, the tax treatment ....[c] Islamic finance transactions and the introduction ....[d] trusts ....[e] French law. (paragraph F)

2 There is increasing interest ....[a] Islamic finance ....[b] the private sector. (paragraph G)

3 The Italian Banking Association and the Union ....[a] Arab Banks entered ....[b] a memorandum ....[c] understanding ....[d] September 2007. (paragraph H)

4 Turkey's Islamic finance sector is tiny, accounting ....[a] less than 5 per cent ....[b] deposits. Turkey has the greatest potential ....[c] expansion ....[d] Islamic finance ....[e] Europe. (paragraph I)

5 The Hong Kong Monetary Authority has formed a working group to put Islamic finance ....[a] an equal basis ....[b] its conventional counterpart. (paragraph K)

OVER TO YOU

1 Using the article as a resource, prepare a five-minute presentation explaining what sharia law is, and illustrating how different countries in the Western world are adapting their regulations so as to attract Islamic finance.

2 Do some research on trusts then write a summary (around 250 words) explaining what they are and how they function. Using a real example can be helpful – for example, find a case where trustees did not carry out their duties satisfactorily, and were taken to court.

Check Test 1 (Units 1–9)

A Use words and phrases from Units 1–9 to complete these sentences.

1 When employees join a company, they are given a c........ o........ e........, which sets out their conditions of work.
2 Companies must c........ w........ strict laws relating to the health and safety of employees.
3 Writing new laws or codes of conduct is known as 'd........'.
4 There is an a........ breach of contract: it has not been proved yet.
5 To avoid the costs and time involved in going to court, disputes can be settled by a........ .
6 After the court h........ was over, the newspapers were able to publish full details of the case.
7 The legal system operating in England and the United States is the c........-l........ system.
8 In court, he made a c........ that he had been treated unfairly by the company.
9 Nowadays, film stars and rock stars need a personal lawyer to r........ them in business dealings.
10 A law firm can also be called a law p........ .
11 If you think you are being discriminated against at work, you can consider f........ a lawsuit against the company.
12 Nowadays, clients want to know about a company's d........ practices – are they offering equal opportunities to all employees?
13 Another name for 'unfair competition laws' is 'a........-t........ laws'.
14 Recent new regulations have b........ smoking in public places.
15 A scam is some kind of f........ activity designed to trick people into paying money to criminals.
16 The number of p........ of Internet criminals has increased, so more of those criminals have been sent to prison as a result.
17 The police arrested a man carrying a case of c........ watches. They were cheap copies of an expensive Swiss-made model.
18 The court f........ the company $25,000 for failing to observe the regulations.
19 Companies must obey not only laws and regulations, but also c........ of practice.
20 This is not a product we designed – we sell it in Europe u........ l........ from the American company that originally produced it.

B Choose the best word or phrase to complete each of these sentences.

1 Companies making products which may be harmful are subject to product .... laws.
a) care b) responsibility c) risk d) liability
2 .... means 'taking action in a court of law'.
a) Legislation b) Litigation c) Complaining d) Processing
3 Lawyers can work in-house, for a company, or privately, for a ....
a) team b) group c) association d) firm
4 Nowadays, large organisations give much thought to the issue of .... social responsibility
a) corporate b) community c) legal d) global

5 'ADR' stands for 'alternative dispute ....'.
 a) reference b) remedies c) resolution d) re-organisation
6 The lawyer .... a previous case, but the judge said it was not relevant.
 a) claimed b) referred c) cited d) stated
7 'Choice of laws' means choosing the most favourable legal .... for settling a dispute.
 a) jurisdiction b) regulations c) court d) judge
8 They had signed a contract, so they had entered .... a legal relationship.
 a) on b) in c) into d) to
9 Some attorneys charge higher .... than others for giving the same advice!
 a) invoices b) fees c) costs d) prices
10 Certain video rights can be .... with the film producer.
 a) vested b) included c) released d) protected
11 When a lawyer acts on behalf of a large number of claimants in one case, this is known as a ....
 a) group case b) representative hearing c) main claim d) class action
12 She is .... of a large US-owned multinational corporation.
 a) law president b) adviser-in-law c) general counsel d) attorney general
13 In a civil claim, the judge can make an award for .... in favour of the claimant.
 a) restoration b) damages c) sentencing d) refunds
14 The court imposed a new .... relating to the way mergers should be regulated in future.
 a) ruling b) order c) direction d) authority
15 This information is not available to the public – it is ....
 a) guarded b) withheld c) secret d) confidential
16 She was very .... about the man's behaviour, so she immediately called the police.
 a) mistrusting b) suspicious c) superstitious d) incredible
17 Protecting copyright falls into the area of .... law.
 a) writers and musicians b) intelligent rights c) intellectual property d) trademark
18 Passing a new law is one thing; successfully .... it is an entirely different matter.
 a) directing b) completing c) demanding d) enforcing
19 The man gave away details of our manufacturing processes – it must be a case for instant .... ! He can't work for us any longer.
 a) unemployment b) retirement c) dismissal d) fire
20 When you buy something in the shops, you have rights under .... laws.
 a) buyers' protection b) customers' rights c) consumer protection d) commercial regulations

Check Test 2 (Units 10–18)

A Use words and phrases from Units 10–18 to complete these sentences.

1 A *c*........ is a group of companies which agree to fix the market price of a product.
2 The three men *p*........ *g*........ to the charge of conspiracy and were each given a prison sentence.
3 We need stricter *a*........-*p*........ legislation to protect the environment properly.
4 They do not admit the charges. In fact, they *d*........ them strongly.
5 Employers have a duty to provide a safe working *e*........ for employees.
6 An employer must provide a *w*........ statement of the company's safety policy. Just telling employees about the policy is not enough.
7 No, it was not in writing. It was an *o*........ agreement.
8 Are you able to *p*........ you are the owner of this car? Do you have any papers, any record of ownership?
9 The contract gives the distributor *e*........ rights to sell these printers in the United States, so no other distributor can sell them there.
10 The manufacturer agrees to *b*........ the cost of delivery to the distributor's warehouse.
11 To *r*........ faulty goods means to refuse to accept those goods.
12 The suppliers did not do what they had agreed to do. There was a clear *b*........ of contract.
13 Switzerland is one of the world's best-known tax *h*........, owing to its banking secrecy practices.
14 Tax *e*........ is illegal. Tax avoidance is legal.
15 Illegally trading company stocks when you have confidential information which could affect the stock price is called '*i*........ *d*........'.
16 In court, he was *s*........ to three years in prison for his part in the crime.
17 The current law is ineffective. It needs to be *r*........ without delay.
18 She will inherit a lot of money, as she is the main *b*........ of her uncle's will.
19 Stealing money from your employer is a criminal *o*........ .
20 If somebody owes you a lot of money, then *s*........ them! Let the court order them to pay!

B Choose the best word or phrase to complete each of these sentences.

1 It was a .... decision in that tax case, one that every tax lawyer will refer to from now on.
a) judicial b) landmark c) financial d) specialised
2 They say it was a cleverly planned fraud. Will they ever catch the .... ?
a) guilty b) performers c) administrators d) perpetrators
3 We don't need to argue that point. It's not ....
a) in case b) to date c) at issue d) on target
4 The proposals should go forward, provided nobody .... them at the last minute.
a) blocks b) disagrees c) overcomes d) passes
5 Employers' duties are not covered in Section 8 of the Act, but in the .... section.
a) above b) preceding c) before-mentioned d) upper

6 This sub-section was .... by a later law, so it is no longer effective.
a) rejected b) cut c) repealed d) repeated

7 Until it's signed by all parties, it's not a .... agreement.
a) legislative b) lawfully relevant c) contracting d) legally binding

8 The new European directive .... clear rules on patent registration procedures.
a) lays down b) lets out c) writes out d) lists down

9 The manufacturer must ensure that the packing of the products .... industry standards.
a) answers b) complies c) meets d) achieves

10 The manufacturer will only accept returned products which are in .... condition.
a) sellable b) selling c) saleable d) re-sale

11 Both .... to the contract realised that the document was not checked before it was signed.
a) bodies b) companies c) societies d) parties

12 When a seller sells a product to a buyer, in English contract law this is known as ....
a) sale of goods b) product sales c) goods contracting d) agreement of sale

13 There are strict laws against money ...., so that companies and individuals cannot easily make illegal profits 'disappear' before tax is paid on them.
a) redirecting b) laundering c) losing d) washing

14 Banks in some countries are required to .... information about customers' bank accounts to tax authorities.
a) hand out b) demonstrate c) disclose d) put up

15 It is not proved yet, but they .... received inside information from contacts in an investment company.
a) alleged b) allegedly c) allegation d) allege

16 Instead of being sent to prison, the company director was given a .... of $50,000.
a) punishment b) fine c) verdict d) caution

17 A .... means all people involved have a fair and equal chance.
a) balanced arena b) well-matched game plan c) level playing field d) flat area

18 The government had to make .... changes to allow the new system to operate within the law.
a) regulatory b) mitigating c) defective d) binding

19 European laws coming out of Brussels are called ....
a) articles b) codes c) directives d) clauses

20 The writer of a published song usually receives a ...., a payment which is a percentage of the sale price of the song.
a) copyright b) royalty c) licence d) subsidy

Answer key

UNIT 1

Reading

A 1 People, products, premises and profit
2 An international cosmetics organisation with offices and factories worldwide

B 1 Medicated skincare products. This is important because these products must comply with strict medicines legislation.
2 Employees, management, shareholders, customers
3 Laws relating to discrimination, diversity and equal opportunities
4 To ensure the product is safe; to describe it accurately in advertising and on packaging
5 What is said in the advertisement, and how it is said
6 Because it needs to protect its rights to patents, trademarks and copyright.
7 Health and safety laws
8 They can use a tax-avoidance scheme.

Vocabulary

A 1 codes 2 under licence from 3 contracts of employment 4 recruited 5 discrimination 6 dismissal 7 shareholders 8 legal status 9 a product liability claim 10 damages 11 legislation 12 breach of contract 13 litigation 14 infringement of patents 15 premises 16 real estate 17 tax evasion

B 1 e 2 d 3 a 4 b 5 c

C 1 equal opportunities 2 criminal offence 3 real estate 4 disciplinary procedure 5 Consumer protection

D 1 1 employment 2 consumer 3 medicines 4 tax 5 health and safety
2 1 under 2 of 3 against 4 with 5 of

UNIT 2

Reading

A 1 Because they can contribute to dealing with widening corporate liability issues and corporate social responsibility matters.
2 For: Philip Rudolph, Elliot Schrage
Against: Bill Carr
3 Clothing, pharmaceuticals

B 1 She no longer needs to justify being at CSR meetings.
2 a) breaches of labour practice codes
b) health concerns about weight problems
3 They can be seen as a valued part of the management team.
4 Lawyers were seen by a third of senior executives to be second only to the CEO in CSR management, and more than 50% of respondents said lawyers should take a leading role in CSR.
5 To see that their clients' standards are met by suppliers
6 Social and environmental risks
7 They may not be able to assess social and environmental issues.
8 They can contribute a rigorous analytical approach because of their training.
9 The issues need to be understood and dealt with, in case they develop into legal problems.

Vocabulary

A 1 'I'm not wearing my legal hat' 2 (general) counsel 3 corporate liability 4 issues 5 codes 6 practice 7 overall 8 drafting 9 third-party 10 contract diligence 11 sweatshop 12 partner 13 objective 14 ethical

B 1 breach 2 compliance 3 to assess 4 to anticipate 5 to respond

C 1 complied 2 response 3 breach 4 assess 5 anticipate

D 1 C 2 D 3 A 4 B 5 D

E 1 a 2 b 3 b 4 a 5 b 6 a

UNIT 3

Reading

A 1 From a study commissioned by PwC
2 No. In fact, many lawyers felt arbitration was expensive.
3 International arbitration

B 1 More flexible procedures, lack of publicity, better chances of enforcement
2 Relatively small disputes
3 Mostly not positive – appeals add time and cost
4 More companies are investing abroad, and the complexity of cross-border disputes is increasing.
5 More common. ICC has over 500 requests annually for arbitration.
6 About 50% are based in Europe, 30% in Asia, 15% in the Americas; most with sales of $500m or more
7 More than 100 in-house lawyers responded.
73% preferred arbitration, with or without other kinds of dispute resolution.
Only 11% favoured litigation. They used special courts or operated in countries with good court systems.
50% said cost was the main concern about arbitration.
Over 60% thought it more expensive than litigation.
23% thought costs were the same as litigation.
91% rejected the idea of allowing appeals in arbitration process.
8 1 Being anxious about foreign law and law courts 2 Cost and time 3 Lack of confidentiality
9 No, they are being challenged more and more.
10 The cost involved

Vocabulary

A 1 b 2 a 3 b 4 b 5 a 6 b 7 b 8 a 9 b 10 b
B 1 c/e 2 d 3 e 4 a 5 b/d
C 1 settle a dispute 2 add costs 3 rejected; argument 4 cited a case 5 law; enforced
D 2 resolved 3 protected 4 oversight 5 consumers 6 represent 7 retain
E 1 for 2 with 3 by 4 to 5 to (*for* is also possible) 6 to

UNIT 4

Reading

A 1 Because people and businesses are looking around for the most appropriate legal systems before they enter into a legal relationship.
2 Choice of laws: choosing a jurisdiction for solving a dispute *before* a dispute arises
Forum shopping: looking for the 'best' jurisdiction *after* a dispute has arisen

B 1 Because they thought they would do better in an English court than in their own country's.
2 No, he thinks it's a strange idea.
3 Financial services
4 English courts strictly interpret the contract as it is written. In America, courts consider the intentions of the parties and how reasonable the contract is.
5 Because of the way the English legal system operates and the fairness of the courts
6 Because judges and juries there are sympathetic to plaintiffs in such cases. It benefits the local community because visiting lawyers bring money to the area.
7 No, it discourages it.

Vocabulary

A 1 a 2 b 3 b 4 b 5 a 6 a 7 b 8 a
B 1 d 2 g 3 e 4 a 5 f 6 h 7 c 8 b
C 1 litigation 2 legal framework 3 libel damages 4 City law firms 5 claimant/plaintiff 6 copyright 7 enter into a legal relationship 8 enforce the terms of the contract
D 1 to defend 2 to determine 3 settlement 4 to resolve 5 transaction 6 to enforce 7 litigation 8 to govern

UNIT 5

Reading

A 1 The film business is far more complicated now – more contracts for more kinds of business, all needing legal advice.
2 Lawyers can't charge such high fees. Not everybody in Bollywood is represented by a lawyer. The contracts are shorter and simpler.

B 1 Because the fees were too high.
2 You have to adapt to the client's needs.
3 Home-entertainment technology and all the legal rights that go with it
4 The contracts did not properly cover the new technology rights.
5 Ring tones on mobile phones, foreign distribution rights, product endorsements
6 Transfer film rights to Mauritius
7 It would be too long and contain too much legal language.
8 Advice on contracts, commercial rights, tax and litigation

Vocabulary

A 1 entertainment law practice 2 high legal fees 3 a standard one-page deal
4 taking [...] to court 5 litigation 6 to determine 7 vested with 8 with no provision for
9 looking at the option of vesting the rights to 10 an aggrieved party 11 legalese 12 comprehensible
B 1 a 2 b 3 a 4 b 5 a 6 a 7 b
C 1 product endorsement 2 clause(s) 3 flourishing 4 cut and pasted 5 precedent 6 stalling 7 rights
D 1 advice 2 fee 3 deal 4 clauses 5 precedents 6 legalese 7 represented 8 litigation

UNIT 6

Reading tasks

A 1 1 Together with the other female divisional general counsel, she was paid less and kept at a lower rank than five male counterparts. Also, women in general are underrepresented in the company's top ranking positions.
2 She moved regularly to a higher position, but had problems reaching the highest levels. This happens to a growing number of businesswomen in the US.
2 1, 3, 5
B 1 T
2 T
3 F (She was told she was not 'big enough' for her job.)
4 F (They make up only 13% of senior corporate officers and 20% of senior band executives.)
5 T
6 F (GE strongly denies the allegations.)
7 T
8 F (Such cases can be harder to bring as class actions because promotion decisions are of a more individual nature.)
C a) The amount of damages being sought
b) The number of upper-level female executives and attorneys at General Electric on whose behalf Ms Schaefer is seeking compensation
c) The percentage of senior corporate officers at GE who are women
d) The percentage of senior band executives at GE who are women
e) The number of years for which Ms Schaefer had worked for GE
f) The year in which GE was given an award for its efforts in increasing the number of female corporate officers

Vocabulary

A 1 filed a lawsuit 2 seeking ($500m in) damages 3 a class action 4 general counsel 5 alleges
6 contend 7 diversity 8 the glass ceiling 9 defend itself 10 an employment attorney
11 represents 12 plaintiffs
B 1 to sue 2 to complain 3 to allege 4 to contend 5 to deny 6 to defend 7 to represent
C 1 allegations 2 denied 3 representation 4 complaint 5 contention 6 sued 7 defend
D 1 D 2 B 3 C 4 A 5 C 6 D
E 1 1 demoted (line 11) 2 denied (line 39)
2 prejudice
3 litigant (gap 4, line 19): a person who brings a lawsuit against someone
litigious (line 21): keen on bringing lawsuits
4 race, sex, disability, age, religious beliefs, sexual orientation

UNIT 7

Reading

A 1 Because Mofcom imposed unexpected restrictions on InBev. Other companies may be cautious of making acquisitions in China because of this.
2 The beer/brewing/breweries industry. InBev cannot acquire (more) shares in these companies.

B 1 1 No (*The first published ruling* ... (line 1))
2 Because it would not harm competition in the home market.
3 InBev is based in Belgium; Anheuser-Busch is based in the USA.
4 Because of the high volume of sales on the Chinese mainland
5 No (... *Mofcom also imposed a number of unanticipated restrictions* ... (lines 21–22))
6 InBev is not allowed to acquire further interests in four key Chinese beer companies.
7 Tsingtao Brewery, Zhujiang Brewery
8 That they should be aware of the new risk presented by this antitrust ruling.
9 Mofcom has imposed future conditions on a deal that did not harm competition.
2 1 F (This is the first ruling of China's new antitrust regime. (paragraph A))
2 F (It was a single-page ruling. (paragraph D))
3 F (InBev cannot increase its shareholding. (paragraph F))
4 T
5 T

Vocabulary

A 1 1 ruling 2 waved through 3 on the grounds that 4 anti-monopoly laws 5 interests 6 broken new ground 7 timely manner
2 1 M&A 2 adversely affect 3 high-profile global deal 4 approval 5 imposed a number of unanticipated restrictions 6 key 7 mergers and acquisitions 8 shareholding, stake 9 banned

B to suffer a defeat
to block a proposal, a decision
to veto a proposal, a decision
to overturn a decision
to uphold a decision

C 1 D 2 B 3 C 4 A 5 D 6 B 7 A

UNIT 8

Reading

A 1 1 He uses it because a real example helps to make the topic clear for the reader.
2 Good progress. There have been many prosecutions, people have been jailed, and some criminal activities have stopped.
2 2 (but only trademarks are mentioned) and 4

B 1 He believed the e-mail was from Microsoft, and the phone call seemed genuine.
2 A handling fee, a tax charge, a $14,600 security deposit and legal fees
3 They have their own internal investigation department of about 65 staff, which investigates every lead.
4 Sending fraudulent e-mails that look like they are from genuine organisations, to try to obtain confidential data
5 Banks use the network to share cybercrime information.
6 To stop the e-mailer sending more e-mails
7 To help evaluate the threat and to provide information for law-enforcement authorities
8 If it is not usual for a company to be targeted by scammers

Vocabulary

A 1 b 2 b 3 a 4 a 5 a 6 a 7 b 8 b

B 1 suspicious 2 police forces 3 lead 4 private detective 5 victims 6 compile 7 arrests 8 prosecutions

C 1 victims 2 arrests; prosecutions 3 suspicious 4 compiled 5 police forces; private detective 6 leads

D 1 1 fraudsters
2 1 a group of people 2 the main part (of a piece of writing)
3 *Suggested answers:* assess, judge
4 A target is something you aim at, e.g. in a shooting competition. The word is used to show how the criminals are focusing directly on a potential victim, their target.
2 1 notify 2 national law enforcement body 3 closure 4 consider

UNIT 9

Reading

A 1 F (*... following a previous complaint from Diageo.* (lines 14–15))
2 F (*The award is unusually high ...* (lines 15–16))
3 F (*... the Chinese authorities are taking counterfeiting much more seriously than in previous years.* (lines 24–27))
4 F (*... as Chinese businessmen become increasingly willing to use the law to protect intangible assets.* (lines 46–48))
5 T

B 1 a 2 b 3 a 4 a 5 b

Vocabulary

A 1 1 counterfeiting 2 damages 3 fined 4 intellectual property rights 5 patent, copyright, trademark 6 guilty verdict 7 suing 8 getting the rulings enforced
2 1 complaint 2 theft 3 court 4 product 5 statement 6 enforce

B 1 damages 2 fine 3 sue 4 intellectual property rights 5 counterfeit 6 enforced 7 guilty verdict 8 trademark

C 1 C 2 D 3 B 4 D 5 C 6 A

D 1 a 2 b

UNIT 10

Reading

A 1 Prosecutors: the three men pleaded guilty.
Defendants: they were able to serve prison sentences in the UK, their home country.
2 CMS Cameron McKenna created a special programme to encourage private businesses and the police to work together against mortgage fraud.
DLA Piper introduced a web-based system to help companies comply with regulations worldwide.

B 1 C 2 C 3 A 4 A 5 B 6 D

Vocabulary

A 1 b 2 a 3 b 4 b 5 a 6 a 7 b 8 b 9 a

B 1 d 2 f 3 g 4 b 5 a 6 c 7 e

C 1 pleaded guilty 2 fix; prices 3 serve a prison sentence 4 recover; losses 5 put together; deal 6 regulations; comply with 7 convicted of a crime

D 1 agreement 2 offence 3 convictions 4 enforcement 5 regulate 6 comply

E 1 of 2 to; in; for 3 to 4 to; of 5 with

UNIT 11

Reading

A 1 They fear that they will have to shut down, because of costs of complying with planned EU legislation.
2 Governments are seriously behind schedule with assessing compliance of plants with this anti-pollution directive, so changes need to be made.
3 Chevron bought Texaco in 2001.
4 This claim is potentially seven times greater than the Exxon Valdez case.

B 1 Those relating to emissions that cause acid rain and smog
2 Tens of thousands of lives may not be saved.
3 They would like to see industry develop innovation and increase investment in clean technologies.
4 The location and design of power stations
5 Because governments are behind schedule in assessing plants for pollution prevention.
6 Because it regulates only one substance at a time.
7 It might become the biggest environmental lawsuit in history.
8 A class action
9 That Texaco did not meet environmental standards
10 It cleaned up oil-well sites as part of a $40m remediation programme.

Vocabulary

A 1 1 to tighten [...] legislation 2 proposals 3 directives 4 anti-pollution measures 5 environmental legislation 6 emission ceilings 7 not at issue 8 contested 9 class action 10 denies the charges 11 remediation agreement 12 declined to comment
2 1 verdict 2 ignore 3 instruct 4 arbitration 5 allege 6 enforce

B 1 1 c 2 d 3 b, d 4 a, d 5 c
2 ... to tighten [...] legislation ... (lines 1–2)
... put forward proposals ... (lines 5–6)
... to toughen directives ... (lines 6–7)
... this right has been abused ... (line 29)
... to tighten standards ... (line 41)
... the proposals [...] not to block them (lines 58–60)

C 1 1 b 2 c 3 a
2 b

D 1 compliance 2 impose 3 eligible 4 backing 5 polluted 6 suit 7 maximise 8 remediation

UNIT 12

Reading

A 1 General duties of employers to their employees in relation to health, safety and welfare at work
2 b
3 It has been repealed by a later Act.

B 1 b
2 Section 2(2)e
3 To provide a written statement of the policy, keep it updated, and let employees know about it
4 To keep health and safety measures under review
5 Section 2(4). The representatives are from amongst the employees.
6 The Genetically Modified Organisms (Contained Use) Regulations 2000.
It relates to an activity involving genetic modification.

Vocabulary

A 1 b 2 b 3 a 4 b 5 a 6 b 7 a 8 b

B 1 in connection with 2 with respect to* 3 in accordance with
* *in respect of* is also grammatically correct, but is not appropriate in this extract from the Act

C 1 1 b 2 a
2 1 Section 2(6): ... any such representatives; ... of such measures.
2 Section 2(7): In such cases as ... ; ... such other functions as ...
3 The representatives already described in Section 2(4); the measures just described (to ensure employees' health and safety at work)
4 1 will 2 may 3 shall

D 1 a) shall b) such c) as 2 shall 3 a) with respect to b) may
4 such 5 may 6 a) in accordance with b) as

UNIT 13

Reading 1

A The existence of an oral agreement can be difficult to prove.

B 1 A piece of paper, something in writing
2 When we buy something from a shop, or get a ticket for a bus or train, or buy chocolate or drinks from a machine
3 A share of the royalties received for the group's music

Vocabulary 1

A 1 satisfy; requirements 2 take; written form 3 deemed; binding contract 4 putting; in writing
5 legal requirements 6 sued 7 oral agreement 8 action failed 9 lack; formalities 10 finding

Reading 2

A It is keen to promote the development of a European Internet industry.

B 1 Contracts to order goods and services from suppliers
2 Explain clearly the steps to be followed to complete the contract online
3 Companies must 1) provide receipts without delay; 2) allow customers to change an order easily; 3) provide details such as business e-mail addresses.
4 Member states must ensure that their laws permit contracts to be made electronically.

Vocabulary 2

A 1 1 c 2 b
2 1 b 2 a
B 1 requirement 2 claim 3 to prove 4 agreement 5 conclusion 6 to comply
C 1 requirements 2 comply 3 conclusion 4 agreement 5 claim 6 prove
D 1 lays down 2 imposes; on

UNIT 14

Reading

A 1 The appointment of the distributor; the term (or period) of the contract; the distributor's rights and duties; shipment of the products; advertising, promotional and product information; payment terms; return of unsold products. (A quick way of finding out is to read the clause headings.)
2 Manufacturer, Distributor, Products, Schedule, Term, Territory. *Agreement* is not usually defined, but a capital letter is used whenever reference is made to the document to be signed by the parties.
B 1 T
2 T
3 F (In Clause 2, Term refers to the period, or duration, of the contract.)
4 F (*The Distributor shall have exclusive distribution in the Territory for the Products.* (Clause 3a))
5 F (*The Manufacturer shall bear the cost of delivery of the Products to the Distributor's shipping agent.* (Clause 4b))
6 T
7 F (*... for which the Distributor shall deem such Products appropriate.* (Clause 5a))
8 F (*The Manufacturer agrees at its sole discretion to accept returns of up to 10% of unsold Products ...* (Clause 7))

Vocabulary

A 1 incorporated in 2 exclusive 3 schedule 4 initial term 5 notice of termination 6 fulfilled 7 bear the cost of 8 meets 9 is obliged to 10 deem 11 sole discretion 12 incurred in
B 1 1 hereto 2 thereof 3 Thereafter
2 1 hereto 2 therein 3 hereby 4 therefor
3 1 a) on b) by c) between
2 a) to b) with c) to d) by
3 a) of b) by c) at d) to
4 a) of b) of c) to d) to
5 a) of b) of c) to d) Upon e) of
6 a) In b) of
7 a) in b) with
C 1 C 2 D 3 B 4 C 5 A 6 C 7 C 8 B

UNIT 15

Reading

A 1 b 2 a 3 b
B 1 A sale of goods contract
2 The contract was for the sale and delivery of special equipment to tow broken-down HGVs.
3 Six months after delivery or on resale, whichever sooner
4 A potential buyer
5 Discussions about rejection started six months after delivery. Actual rejection was after 13 months (July 1997).
6 The time expected to be needed for resale, plus extra time for the sub-purchaser to inspect and test
7 A month or two, perhaps plus time to discuss putting defects right
8 The defendants

Vocabulary

A 1 1 claimant(s); defendant(s) 2 contracted 3 the essence of the contract 4 breached 5 comply with 6 rejecting 7 the parties 8 defects
2 1 sale of goods 2 delivery 3 guidelines 4 specifications 5 whichever 6 sub-purchaser
B 1 f 2 c 3 g 4 a 5 e 6 d 7 b
C 1 ab initio 2 per se 3 subpoena 4 bona fide; caveat emptor 5 ultra vires 6 ad hoc 7 affidavit 8 ex gratia 9 inter alia

UNIT 16

Reading

A 1 Singapore's banking laws are strict; the tax laws are favourable.
2 Because of the unfavourable requirements of the EU Savings Directive
3 Bank secrecy, no law against tax evasion, no tax on global income

B 1 F (It said that *banks in tax sanctuaries such as Switzerland must impose withholding taxes on accounts held by EU citizens if the names of the account holders are not revealed.* (lines 8–13))
2 T
3 T
4 F (*Singapore has been much more restrictive than the UK in the exchange of information ...* (lines 40–42))
5 T
6 F (*But Singapore is under growing pressure from foreign governments to disclose more information about local bank accounts ...* (lines 58–61))
7 T
8 F (*An aggressive enforcement of the rules would probably drive away some private banks.* (lines 93–95))

Vocabulary

A 1 tax haven, low-tax jurisdiction, tax sanctuary 2 to reveal, to disclose 3 current law 4 foreign jurisdictions 5 inherited 6 intermediary 7 banning 8 laundering 9 illegal activities 10 financial fraud

B 1 a 2 b 3 b 4 a 5 b 6 a 7 a

C 1 tax haven 2 wealth management 3 withholding tax 4 bank secrecy 5 Tax evasion 6 income tax; corporate tax 7 common-law 8 double-taxation treaty

D 1 signature 2 to evade 3 avoidance 4 disclosure 5 to ban 6 demand 7 assistance 8 refusal

UNIT 17

Reading

A 1 They are taking legal action against insider dealers and handing down substantial prison sentences.
2 He was an analyst / a research associate. Professional traders (in hedge funds, for example) present the biggest difficulties.

B 1 individuals: lines 1–6; groups: lines 11–14
2 b
3 He did it in an unsophisticated way. / It was highly unusual / seemingly unsophisticated.
4 To illustrate how unsophisticated Mr Plotkin's scheme was
5 b
6 To highlight (further) the lack of sophistication
7 He spoke to an analyst from Merrill Lynch and a grand juror in New Jersey; he hired strippers to get information from investment bankers; he conspired with two employees of a printing plant (who stole advance copies of *BusinessWeek*) and a former Goldman employee, David Pajcin.
8 To protect his position – he is not certain these are proven facts.

Vocabulary

A 1 sentence 2 crackdown 3 illicit 4 sophisticated 5 defence attorney 6 former 7 prosecutor 8 allegedly 9 gossip 10 pleaded guilty 11 grand juror 12 to hire 13 merger 14 pending 15 acquisition

B 1 to sentence 2 reminder 3 prosecutor 4 prosecution 5 to retire 6 investor 7 investment/investing 8 investigator 9 investigation 10 to allege

C 1 investment 2 retired 3 prosecution 4 was investigated 5 reminder 6 sentence 7 prosecutor 8 alleged 9 investors 10 investigation

D 1 may/might/could 2 take 3 because/as/since 4 exchange/return 5 different

E 1 monitoring 2 turmoil 3 regulator 4 swings 5 policing 6 immunity

UNIT 18

Reading

A 1 Because it is an alternative source of funds in a relatively healthy condition.
2 Through tax and regulatory changes, particularly in the financial sector

B 1 Capital must be used in a genuine commercial activity.
Full disclosure is required so that the nature of any contract is absolutely clear.
2 Because conventional indexes lost more than 20 per cent.
3 Record oil prices
4 It has authorised six Islamic banks.
5 France: listing of sukuk, tax in relation to Islamic financial transactions, introduction of trusts
Germany: the issue of Europe's first Islamic bond, use of takaful
6 Despite having a significant Muslim population, Turkey is run as a secular state.
7 Singapore

Vocabulary

A 1 liquidity 2 toxic 3 suffered 4 a level playing field 5 gilt 6 listing 7 private sector
8 subsidiaries 9 launched 10 intermediary

B 1 1 regulatory changes 2 to review 3 trusts 4 a memorandum of understanding 5 quasi
6 amended
2 1 trustee, settlor, beneficiary
2 fiduciary
3 In a living trust, the settlor is alive; in a testamentary trust, the settlor has died.
4 A will
5 A trust instrument (or trust deed)
6 No. They have a duty to invest with care.

C reformation (line 18), amended (line 105)

D 1 change 2 to reform 3 amendment 4 variation 5 to modify 6 alteration

E 1 a) to b) of c) of d) of e) into
2 a) in b) from
3 a) of b) into c) of d) in
4 a) for b) of c) for d) of e) in
5 a) on b) with

CHECK TEST 1

A 1 contract of employment 2 comply with 3 drafting 4 alleged 5 arbitration 6 hearing
7 common-law 8 claim 9 represent 10 practice 11 filing 12 diversity 13 anti-trust
14 banned 15 fraudulent 16 prosecutions 17 counterfeit 18 fined 19 codes
20 under licence

B 1 d 2 b 3 d 4 a 5 c 6 c 7 a 8 c 9 b 10 a 11 d 12 c 13 b 14 a 15 d
16 b 17 c 18 d 19 c 20 c

CHECK TEST 2

A 1 cartel 2 pleaded guilty 3 anti-pollution 4 deny 5 environment 6 written 7 oral
8 prove 9 exclusive 10 bear 11 reject 12 breach 13 havens 14 evasion
15 insider dealing 16 sentenced 17 reviewed 18 beneficiary 19 offence 20 sue

B 1 b 2 d 3 c 4 a 5 b 6 c 7 d 8 a 9 c 10 c 11 d 12 a 13 b 14 c 15 b
16 b 17 c 18 a 19 c 20 b

Glossary

A

absence *n.* when something is not there, is not present

abuse *v.* to deliberately use something for the wrong purpose or for your own advantage

access *n.* a way into a place, building or system

acquisition *n.* when one company buys another one, or part of another one

act *n.* a law that has been officially accepted by the governing body of a country; in Britain, an Act of Parliament

action *n.* the process of taking a case or a claim against someone to a court of law

adapt *v.* to change something to make it suitable for a different purpose

adequate *adj.* enough in quantity or of a good enough quality for a particular purpose

admit *v.* To *admit* to a crime or offence is to state in court that you accept a criminal charge is correct.

adopt *v.* If you *adopt* a new method, process, etc. you start to use it.

ADR (alternative dispute resolution) *n.* methods of settling legal disagreements without using an ordinary court

adversely *adv.* unfavourably, negatively

affirm *v.* to confirm that something is correct

aggrieved *adj.* having suffered as a result of the illegal actions of someone else

allegation *n.* a statement that someone has done something wrong or illegal, but that has not been proved

alleged *adj.* An *alleged* crime, fact, etc. is one that someone says has happened or is true, although it has not been proved.

amend *v.* to make changes to a law or a document, e.g. to improve it, to make it more accurate or to take account of new conditions

anticipate *v.* to expect that something will happen and be ready for it

antitrust *adj.* relating to laws in the USA that make it illegal for a company or group of companies to restrict competition, set up a monopoly or limit another person's freedom to run a business

appeal *v.* to make a formal request to a higher court or authority for a decision made by a lower court, committee, etc. to be changed

arbitration *n.* when a legal disagreement is dealt with by independent officials who have the authority to make a legal decision about it, rather than the case being dealt with in a court of law

arrest *n.* when the police take someone and keep them under police control, because they may have done something illegal

aspect *n.* one part of a situation, idea, plan, etc. that has many parts

attorney *n.* (US) a lawyer, especially one who represents clients and speaks in court

award *n.* an amount of money that is given to someone as a result of an official decision or judgment. A court gives an award.

award *v.* to officially decide that someone should have something such as an amount of money

B

backing *n.* support or help

ban *v.* to say officially that something must not be done, used, etc.

barrister *n.* a lawyer (especially in England) who usually specialises in a particular field of law, gives legal opinions and is qualified to present a case in court

bear the cost *v.* pay / be responsible for the cost

before the event before an event of legal relevance has taken place

beneficiary *n.* someone whose property is looked after by a trustee, or who receives money or property in a will

bias *n.* not a neutral view or opinion, but favouring one party or group, etc.; prejudice (often seen as unfair)

binding contract *n.* a contract that courts of law will recognise as legal

board *n.* the group of people who have been elected to manage a company by those holding shares in the company

bond *n.* a document promising to pay back money borrowed by a government or company, usually with interest

breach of contract *n.* when someone fails to do something that they have agreed to do in a contract

break new ground *v.* to do something new, something not done before

brewery *n.* a company that makes and sells beer, or a factory where beer is made

bring a suit *v.* to sue; to file a lawsuit; to take civil proceedings against someone

bring into force *v.* When a law is *brought into force*, it begins to work, to operate.

bring something to the notice of someone *v.* to inform someone, to bring something to their attention

C

cartel *n.* a group of companies who agree to set the price of something they produce at a fixed level in order to limit competition and increase their own profits

case *n.* a question or problem that is dealt with by a court of law

charge *n.* an official statement saying that someone has done something against the law

chassis *n.* the frame on which the body, engine, wheels, etc. of a vehicle are built

choice of laws *n.* deciding on which country's legal system to use to resolve a dispute, before any dispute has occurred

cite *v.* to mention something as an example, especially in order to support, prove or explain what you are saying

City law firms *n.pl.* (UK) large firms of solicitors in the City of London, the business district

civil code *n.* a written set of laws of a country

civil law *n.* as a legal system, the law of ancient Rome, which is still used as the basis for the legal system in some countries, especially the countries of continental Europe or countries formerly governed by them. Civil law relates to peoples' rights; crimes, on the other hand, are dealt with by criminal law.

claim *n.* a legal demand for compensation following a dispute, an accident, breach of a right, etc.

claimant *n.* someone who makes a civil claim in court (see also plaintiff)

class action *n.* when a group of people who have all suffered in the same way take a person or organisation to court together

clause *n.* A contract is divided into *clauses*, often referred to by subject, e.g. the Definitions *Clause*, the Payments *Clause*, etc.

code *n.* **1** a set of rules and regulations for a particular industry. A *code* of practice states how companies should be run correctly. These codes do not usually have the force of law. **2** a complete set of written rules or laws (see **civil code**)

commission *v.* to formally ask someone to produce a report, work of art, etc.

commit *v.* to do, to carry out (e.g. an offence, a crime)

common law *n.* law that has been developed from common customs and the decisions of judges rather than being decided by an Act of Parliament or an Act of Congress

compile *v.* to collect information together and write it into a list, report, book, etc.

compliance *n.* when companies follow laws and regulations strictly

comply *v.* If a company *complies* with a law, it obeys it.

concerns *n.pl.* worries, feelings that something is wrong

conclude *v.* to come to agreement about all points (in a contract)

conclusion *n.* The conclusion of a contract is when all points are agreed.

conditions *n.pl.* something stated in a contract, agreement or insurance policy that must be done or must be true otherwise the contract, agreement, or policy will be ended or will not remain in force

confidential *adj. Confidential* information is spoken or written in private and intended to be kept secret.

confidentiality *n.* the practice of keeping private information secret

conglomerate *n.* a large business organisation consisting of several different companies that have joined together

consent *n.* willing agreement to a contract and its conditions, without any force or dishonesty having been used

consortium *n.* a combination of several companies, banks, etc. working together for a particular purpose, e.g. in order to buy something or build something

conspiracy *n.* a plan made by two or more people or companies to do something illegal. Conspiracy to commit a crime is itself a crime.

consumer *n.* a person who buys goods, products and services for their own use, not for business use or to resell

consumer protection laws to protect people when they have bought goods or services, covering things such as price, quality or safety

contend *v.* to argue or state that something is true

contest *v.* to state that you do not accept something or do not agree with it

contract *v.* to formally agree to do something, e.g. by signing a contract

contract of employment *n.* a formal document giving the conditions of someone's job, how much they are paid, etc.

convict *v.* Someone who is convicted of a crime is found guilty of that crime.

conviction *n.* **1** a decision in a court of law that someone is guilty of a crime **2** the process of proving someone guilty in a court of law

copyright *n.* a legal right which a writer, musician, artist, film maker, etc. has in their own work, so that it cannot be copied or reproduced without payment of royalties. The right can be licensed to another person or company.

corporate social responsibility (CSR) *n.* the idea that businesses should consider the public interest (the environment, consumer welfare, etc.) in their plans and actions, no matter whether they are legally required to do so

corporate lawyer *n.* a lawyer who advises companies in business matters

corporate liability *n.* the legal responsibility of a company to obey the law

counsel *n.* **1** (UK) a barrister who represents a client in a court of law **2** a lawyer or group of lawyers who give legal advice to a company or organisation

counter *v.* to fight against

counterfeit *v.* to illegally copy a product

counterfeit *adj.* illegally copied or made to look exactly like a genuine product

counterpart *n.* Your counterpart is another person who has the same job or level of responsibility as you.

criminal offence *n.* an act which is against the law; a crime

cross-border disputes *n.pl.* arguments about legal matters between companies based in different countries

crucially *adv.* very importantly, of key significance

D

damages *n.pl.* in a civil claim, money that a court orders the defendant to pay to the claimant as financial compensation for harming them or their property, or causing them financial loss

decision *n.* the court's judgment in a civil court

decline to comment *v.* to choose to say nothing about a situation

deem *v.* If something is *deemed* to be, e.g. a binding contract, it is considered to be a binding contract.

defect *n.* a fault in something that means it is not perfect

defence *n.* **1** the things that are said in a court of law to try to prove that someone is not guilty of a crime **2** the lawyers in a court of law who try to prove that someone is not guilty of a crime

defend *v.* If a lawyer *defends* someone charged with a crime, he or she represents that person and argues that they are not guilty of the charge.

defendant *n.* the person or organisation in a court of law that has been accused of doing something illegal

deny *v.* in court, to say that a claim or charge is not true (the opposite of admit)

depressed *adj.* An economy or industry that is *depressed* does not have enough manufacturing or business activity.

derive *v.* to receive, usually from a particular source

determine *v.* to decide the exact meaning of the conditions of a contract, e.g. when there are disagreements about it

deterrent *n.* something, usually a punishment, that makes someone less likely to do something, by making them realise it will have bad results

diligence *n.* the care and attention required, e.g. when checking that details of a contract comply with the law

disability *n.* a physical problem that makes someone unable to use a part of their body

disciplinary procedure *n.* in a company, the official way to warn an employee that they are breaking rules or working unacceptably

disclose *v.* to make something publicly known, especially after it has been kept confidential

discretion *n.* When a party to a contract, or a judge, does something at their *discretion*, they have the freedom to choose to do it.

discriminate *v.* To *discriminate* against a person or group of people is to act unfairly towards them. In legal matters, this is generally because of race, nationality, sex, religious belief, age, etc.

discrimination *n.* when a worker in a company is treated unfairly because of their race, sex, age, etc, especially by not being considered for a job. This is illegal in many countries.

dismissal *n.* when someone is removed from their job by their employer

disproportionate *adj.* too much or too little in relation to something else

diversity *n.* in employment law, giving equal opportunities to employees from minority groups (e.g. people with physical disabilities, people from minority religious or ethnic groups)

divest *v.* to reduce the number of your investments by selling some of them

double-taxation treaty *n.* an agreement between different tax authorities to avoid a person or company being taxed twice when the same income is taxable in two countries or states

draft *v.* to write/prepare a document / a contract / some legislation that has to be checked and possibly changed, and so is not yet in its finished form

E

egress *n.* a way out of a building or place; an exit

eligible *adj.* can be chosen to do something or receive something

elusive *adj.* An *elusive* idea or quality is difficult to describe or understand.

emerge *v.* to begin to be known or noticed. e.g. an emerging nation

encounter *v.* to meet something, especially problems or opposition

enforce *v.* to make sure something is done (an award is paid out, a debt paid), or is obeyed (a law, a rule)

enforcement *n.* when people are made to obey a rule, law, etc.

ensure *v.* to make certain that something will happen properly

enter into a contract *v.* to become a party to a contract

enter into a legal relationship *v.* to begin business and other dealings that are governed by the law

enterprise *n.* a company or business; a commercial organisation

entitle *v.* When someone is *entitled* to do something, they have the right to do it.

envisage *v.* to think that something is likely to happen in the future

equal opportunities *n.pl.* when the same chances and opportunities for employment are given to everyone whatever their age, sex, race, religion, etc.

essence *n.* in contract law, the most important part of a contract, without which no agreement would have been made

ethical *adj.* **1** connected with principles of what is right and wrong **2** morally good or correct

EU directives *n.pl.* laws of the European Union, affecting Member States of the EU

evaluate *v.* to carefully consider something to see how important it is

evidence *n.* information or facts given in a court of law to prove that someone is guilty

exclusive *adj.* An *exclusive* agreement, contract or right is one that a single person or organisation has and no one else has.

F

faulty *adj.* If a machine, system, etc. is *faulty*, there is something wrong with it that prevents it from working correctly.

fee *n.* an amount of money paid to a professional person or organisation for their services

fictional *adj.* *Fictional* people, events, etc. are imaginary.

fictitious *adj.* not true; not real

fiduciary *adj.* involving confidence, trust

file *v.* to officially record a complaint, law case, official document, etc.

find *v.* to make a legal decision after hearing a case, e.g. The court *found* the accused guilty of the offence.

fine *v.* to punish an offender by ordering them to pay a sum of money

fine *n.* money that someone has to pay as a punishment for an offence

firm *n.* Lawyers and other professionals can work in a partnership, called a *firm*.

follow suit *v.* to do the same thing; to follow the example

for the time being (also **for the present**) **1** at the relevant time, at that time, then **2** for the present

former *adj.* A *former* detective means that person was a detective in the past, but is not one now.

forum shopping *n.* finding a favourable jurisdiction for a court hearing after a dispute has occurred

fraud *n.* a method of illegally getting money from a person or organisation, often using clever and complicated methods

fraudster *n.* someone who has committed a fraud

fraudulent *adj.* *Fraudulent* activities, documents, etc. are intended to deceive.

freedom of contract *n.* the idea that parties to a contract are, generally speaking, free to include whatever obligations they like in a contract

fulfil *v.* to do the things that a law, a contract or some other authority says you must do

G

general counsel *n.* **1** the chief legal officer of a US company **2** a firm of US lawyers that gives general legal advice

gilt *n.* British government bond

glass ceiling *n.* the attitudes in an organisation that prevent women from rising beyond a certain level, despite having the necessary skills and ability

globalisation *n.* the tendency for the world economy to work as one unit, led by large international companies doing business all over the world.

govern *v.* If rules, principles, etc. *govern* the way a system or organisation works, they control how things are done.

governance *n.* regulation and control of how something operates

grand juror *n.* (US) a responsible citizen chosen to sit on a jury to decide if someone should be charged with a crime

grant *v.* to officially give a person or an organisation something they have asked for

groundbreaking *adj.* *Groundbreaking* work involves making new discoveries, using new methods, etc.

grounds *n.pl.* a reason, often a legal or official one, for doing or believing something

guidelines *n.pl.* instructions on how people should do or deal with something

guilty *adj.* having done something that is a crime (opposite of **innocent**)

H

hacker *n.* someone who secretly reaches information on someone else's computer system so that they can look at, use or change it

hacking *n.* secretly obtaining information on someone else's computer system so that you can look at, use or change it

hand down *v.* in court, to give / to deliver a decision

hear *v.* to listen to all the facts in a case in a court of law in order to make a legal decision

hearing *n.* a meeting of a court or special committee to find out the facts about a case

hedge funds *n.pl.* a fund that makes investments that are unlikely to fall in value, as well as in those that go up or down in value, to reduce the risk of losing a lot of money

HR department *n.* the Human Resources department of a company, responsible for employing, training and, if necessary, dismissing employees

I

illicit *adj.* not allowed by laws or rules; strongly disapproved of by society

immunity *n.* the state or right of being protected from particular laws

implication *n.* a possible future effect or result of an action, event, decision, etc.

impose *v.* to officially put in place an order that something should be restricted, forbidden, taxed, etc.

in conjunction with together with

incorporated *adj.* formed as a legal registered company

in the event of if something should happen

incur *v.* If you *incur* expenses, costs or a debt, you become responsible for paying them.

inevitably *adv.* used for saying that something is certain to happen and cannot be avoided

inflict *v.* to make someone suffer something unpleasant

infringement *n.* something that is against a law or someone's legal rights, particularly intellectual property rights

ingredient *n.* the substance in a product such as a medicine that causes the product's intended result

inherit *v.* **1** to receive money or property from someone after they have died, usually through a will **2** to receive something from someone or something there before you, e.g. to inherit a problem

in-house lawyer *n.* a lawyer who is employed by a company, rather than working independently or for a law firm

innocent *adj.* not guilty of a crime

insider dealing (also **insider trading**) *n.* when someone uses knowledge of a particular company, situation, etc. that is not available to other people in order to buy or sell shares. It is an illegal practice.

intangible asset *n.* something that a business has and can make money from, but that is not something physical and so cannot easily be valued, e.g. a name of a product, a trademark, technical knowledge, loyalty from customers, etc.

intellectual property *n.* an idea, design or artistic work which a person or organisation has invented or created and has rights in, such as a copyright, trademark or patent

interests *n.pl.* shares that you own in a company, or a part of a company that a person or organisation owns

intermediary *n.* a person or organisation that helps to arrange agreements or business deals between other people or organisations

interpret *v.* to explain the meaning of a law or precedent

intimate *v.* to make known; to inform

invalid *adj.* An *invalid* contract, agreement, document, etc. is not legally or officially acceptable.

issue *n.* a matter for discussion; a problem

J

judgment *n.* a decision made by a court of law

judicial *adj.* connected with a court of law or the legal system

jurisdiction *n.* the extent of legal power a particular court, or country's court, has

jury *n.* a group of ordinary people, often 12 in number, who listen to details of a case in court and decide on it

L

landmark *adj.* A *landmark* agreement, decision, settlement, etc. is one that is very important and influences how other things develop.

launch *v.* to show or make a new product available for sale for the first time

law report *n.* an official record of legal cases, used to help lawyers decide on a particular course of action

lawsuit *n.* a charge, claim or complaint against someone that is made in a court of law by a private person or company, not by the police or state

lay down *v.* to state; to establish

lead *n.* a clue, some information to help solve a crime

legal proceedings *n.pl.* a lawsuit, legal action in court

legalese *n.* language used by lawyers that many people find difficult to understand

legislation *n.* **1** a law or set of laws **2** the act of making laws

legitimate *adj.* operating according to the law

level playing field *n.* a situation in which different companies, countries, etc. can all compete fairly with each other because no one has special advantages

liability *n.* **1** risk **2** the responsibility that a person or organisation has for loss, damage or injury caused to others, or for payment of debts

liable *adj.* legally responsible for something

libel *n.* when someone writes or prints untrue statements about someone so that other people could have a bad opinion of them

licence *n.* **1** permission to produce, sell or use the name of a product belonging to another company **2** a document giving permission to do something

liquidity *n.* the amount of readily available money in an economy at a particular time

listing *n.* when a company is on an official list of shares which can be bought on a particular stock market

litigant *n.* someone who is making a claim against a person or company in a court of law

litigation *n.* when someone makes a claim or complaint against a person or organisation in a court of law

litigious *adj.* very willing or too willing to take complaints to a court of law

logo *n.* a design or way of writing its name that a company or organisation uses as its official sign on its products, advertising, etc. A marketing term rather than a legal one.

loot *v.* to steal money or valuable goods

M

mainstream *n.* the people whose ideas about a subject are shared by most people and regarded as normal

make a claim *v.* to start a court action by saying you have a legal right to something; to take legal proceedings against someone

maximise *v.* to increase something such as profit or income as much as possible

measure *n.* an official action, taken to deal with a particular problem

mechanism *n.* a system used to achieve something or deal with a problem

mediation *n.* a way of trying to end a dispute between two people or groups by talking to both sides and encouraging them to reach an agreement. An alternative to going to court.

meet *v.* to achieve a level that has been set or expected

memorandum of understanding *n.* a document signed by two or more organisations to say that they are willing to work together, perhaps before a more detailed contract is signed

merger *n.* when two or more companies join together to form a larger company

misconduct *n.* in employment law, the incorrect or dishonest behaviour of an employee

mislead *v.* to make someone believe something that is not true by giving them information that is false or not complete

mitigate *v.* to reduce the effects of something

mitigating circumstances *n.pl.* things which can make a crime less serious, or excuse it

mitigation *n.* If you say something in *mitigation*, you try to make someone's crime or mistake seem less serious or show that they were not completely responsible.

modification *n.* a change made in something such as a law, design, plan or system

money laundering *n.* when money that has been obtained illegally is put into legal businesses or bank accounts in different countries, so that it is difficult for people to discover where it came from

monitor *v.* to carefully watch and check a situation in order to see how it changes or progresses over a period of time

monopoly *n.* a situation where a business activity is controlled by only one company or by the government, and other companies do not compete with it

mortgage *n.* a legal arrangement where you borrow money from a financial institution in order to buy land or a house, and you pay back the money over a period of years.

N

not at issue not disputed; all parties accept the fact

notice of termination *n.* advance information saying you wish to end something, e.g. a contract, a job, a rental agreement

notion *n.* an idea, belief or opinion

O

obliged to do something *v.* when you must do something because of laws, rules, terms of a contract

oral contract *n.* a spoken contract. It is not written down.

outcome *n.* the final result of a meeting, discussion, court case, etc.

out of line *adj.* not following the usual direction, way of thinking, acting, etc.

oversee *v.* to organise and control an activity or the work that people or an organisation do

oversight *n.* supervision; keeping a watch on or control over something

overturn *v.* to change a court decision, usually so that it becomes the opposite of what it was before

P

panel *n.* a group of people chosen to give advice or decide something

parole *n.* permission for someone to leave prison, on the condition that they promise to behave well

party *n.* the people or group of people involved in a legal case, dispute, contract, etc.

pass *v.* When a law is *passed*, it is authorised by a governing body.

passing off *n.* pretending that a product is someone else's in order to cheat people. Usually a cheaply manufactured product is made to look very similar to a well-known, expensive one.

patent *n.* a legal document giving a person or company the right to make or sell a new invention, product or method of doing something and stating that no other person or company is allowed to do this

pending *adj.* about to happen; waiting to take place

perennial *adj.* happening again and again; continuing or existing for a long time

perpetrator *n.* someone who does something illegal or morally wrong

personnel *n.* the people who work for a company or organisation

piracy *n.* the illegal copying of books, CDs, videos, etc.

pirate *v.* to illegally copy copyrighted work

plaintiff *n.* someone who brings a civil action against someone in a court of law (also **claimant**)

plant *n.* a factory or building where an industrial process takes place or a product is made

plea bargaining *n.* when someone agrees to admit in court that they are guilty of one crime, in exchange for not being charged with a more serious crime

plead guilty *v.* to respond to a criminal charge in court by stating you are guilty

police *v.* to control a particular activity or industry by making sure that people follow the correct rules

police force *n.* the official police organisation in a country or area

practicable *adj.* can be done; can be carried out or put into practice

practice *n.* the business or place of work of a lawyer, doctor, etc. or a group of lawyers, doctors, etc.

precedent *n.* **1** a contract or part of a contract that has been used successfully before, and so can be used again for a similar situation **2** a court decision which can be used later to support another legal decision

preceding *adj.* coming before the part, place or time mentioned

prejudice *n.* **1** an unreasonable dislike of people because they are different from you in some way, especially because of their race, sex or religious beliefs **2** bias; an unreasonable opinion about something or dislike of it

premises *n.pl.* the buildings and land used by a business, shop, hotel, etc.

prescribe *v.* to specify officially, e.g. prescribed by law

price-fixing *n.* when companies in an industry agree on the prices they will charge for something. This form of price-fixing is done so that companies avoid competing with each other, and is normally illegal.

principal *adj.* main; most important

prior to *adv.* before (in time)

private sector *n.* the industries and services that are not owned by the government

product endorsement *n.* when a well-known person says in an advertisement how good they think a product is

product liability *n.* when the maker of a product is responsible for any damage or injury that the product causes

proof *n.* evidence (facts, concrete information) that shows something is true

property *n.* land and buildings (US real estate)

prosecution *n.* **1** the process or act of bringing a charge against someone for a crime, or of being judged for a crime in a court of law **2** the lawyers in a court of law who try to prove that someone is guilty of a crime

prosecutor *n.* a lawyer who represents the authorities in bringing a criminal charge against someone

prove *v.* to show that something is true by providing facts, information, etc.

provision *n.* a legal condition, in a contract or a law

Q

quasi- *prefix* seems like, or is almost, something else, but it is not that thing

R

real estate *n.* (US) land or buildings

reassure *v.* to make someone feel calmer and less worried or frightened about a problem or situation

rebate *n.* an amount of money that is paid back to you when you have paid too much

recruit *v.* to find new people to work for an organisation, do a job, etc.

registered design *n.* a design which has been registered to give protection against illegal copying

registered office *n.* (UK) the official address of a company where all letters and notices must be sent. By law, every British company must have a *registered office*.

regulate *v.* to control with rules; to govern how something operates

regulations *n.pl.* laws, rules and orders made by national and local authorities

reject *v.* to not accept an idea, a proposal, a thing; e.g. in a sale of goods, to refuse to accept a product because its quality is not good enough

remediation *n.* efforts to put things right after damage or harm has been suffered, by paying compensation or taking special action

remedy *n.* in law, a way of repairing harm or damage suffered

repeal *v.* to officially end a law, rule, restriction, etc.

reputation *n.* **1** the opinion people have of something (e.g. a company) or someone, based on what has happened in the past **2** a good name, e.g. to have a reputation for being fair

resent *v.* to feel angry or upset about a situation or about something that someone has done

resolution *n.* finding the answer to a problem, the solution to a dispute

resolve *v.* to find a satisfactory way of settling a disagreement, dispute, etc.

restriction *n.* an official rule that limits or controls what people can do or what is allowed to happen

retain *v.* to keep something or to continue to have it

reveal *v.* to make known something that was previously secret or unknown

revise *v.* to change a piece of writing, a decision, an opinion by adding new information, making improvements or correcting mistakes

rights *n.pl.* **1** benefits given by law, e.g. the right of a consumer to expect that a product will do what it is designed to do **2** freedom to use powers given by law

rigidity *n.* being firmly fixed, with no flexibility

risk management *n.* the managing of the risks related to a company's activities in a way that limits possible financial losses and other kinds of damage to the company

royalties *n.pl.* a payment made to someone who owns a copyright or a patent, e.g. the writer of a book or an inventor. The amount depends on the number of products or copies of the work which are sold.

ruling *n.* an official decision, especially one made by a court

S

sale of goods *n.* a specific area of contract law relating to the sale of goods, rather than land, intellectual property, etc.

saleable *adj.* Something that is *saleable* can be sold.

scam *n.* a clever but dishonest plan, usually to get money

scheme *n.* a plan or arrangement

seek *v.* to ask for, e.g. to seek damages

sentence *v.* to send someone to prison as a punishment for a crime

sentence *n.* a punishment that a judge gives to someone who is guilty of a crime

serve a prison sentence *v.* to spend time in prison

serve notice on someone *v.* to give someone official information, usually in a specified way, e.g. personally, by hand, by post, etc.

settle *v.* to end an argument by agreeing to do something

settlement *n.* an agreement after a dispute, especially about distribution of money and property, e.g. a divorce settlement

settlor *n.* a person who gives property or goods to someone under an agreement, often a will

sexual orientation *n.* the fact that someone is heterosexual or homosexual

shall *v.* used in contracts and official documents to state an order, law, promise, etc. It indicates you are obliged to do something.

share *n.* a part of a company which can be owned, e.g. You can buy and sell *shares* in Company A.

shareholder *n.* someone who owns shares in a company

shareholding *n.* a quantity of shares in a company held by a particular person or organisation

shortcomings *n.pl.* a fault or weakness that makes someone or something less successful or effective than they should be

smog *n.* dirty air caused by pollution from factories and vehicles in cities

sole *adj.* A *sole* responsibility, duty, right, etc. is one that is not shared with anyone else

solely *adv.* not involving anything or anyone else

solicitor *n.* (UK) a lawyer who gives legal advice to members of the public and to companies and can represent them in court

stake *n.* money invested or risked in a business

stall *v.* to delay something or someone, usually intentionally

standard contract *n.* a printed contract containing the usual clauses for an agreement of that type

standards *n.pl.* in commerce and industry, levels of quality that must be met, e.g. advertising standards, building standards

statute *n.* a written law; (UK) an Act of Parliament

statutory *adj.* fixed or controlled by law

strike a balance *v.* to find an acceptable point between opposite views, ideas, systems

subject to *adj.* **1** under the control of, e.g. Commercial sellers are *subject to* legal supervision. **2** depending on, conditional on, e.g. The offer is accepted, *subject to* the Board's approval.

subsidiary *n.* a company that is at least half-owned by another company

substance *n.* material, e.g. Factories can contain dangerous *substances*.

sue *v.* to make a legal claim against someone in a civil court, especially for an amount of money, because you have been harmed in some way

suspect *n.* someone who the police believe has committed a crime

suspicious *adj.* feeling that you do not trust someone or something

sustainability *n.* the idea of being able to protect natural resources and take care of the environment

sweatshop *n.* a small business, factory, etc. where people work very hard in poor conditions for very low pay

T

tackle *v.* to try to deal with a difficult problem

take someone to court *v.* to start legal proceedings against someone

take something into account *v.* to take into consideration; to see as being important

takeover *n.* the act of getting control of a company by buying over 50% of its shares

target *v.* to choose someone or something for a particular type of treatment, e.g. The company targeted teenagers during the launch of their new sportswear range.

tax avoidance *n.* legal ways of paying less tax

tax evasion *n.* illegal ways of paying less tax

tax haven *n.* a place where people go to live or to invest money, in order to avoid paying high taxes in their own country

term *n.* **1** one of the conditions of an agreement or contract **2** the period of time that an agreement or legal right continues for

terms and conditions *n.pl.* the basis for agreement between contracting parties

thereby *adv.* **1** by doing that; in that way **2** in contracts and legislation, 'by that', e.g. The manufacturer is *thereby* released from all obligations.

third party *n.* **1** someone other than the main parties involved, often someone outside the company or organisation **2** someone who is not one of the two main people or organisations involved in an agreement or legal case

timely *adv.* done or happening at exactly the right time

track *v.* to follow the progress of

trade union *n.* an organisation representing people working in a particular industry or profession that protects their rights

trademark (also **trade mark**) *n.* a name, symbol or design used on a product to show it is made by a particular company; when registered, it can be protected from illegal copying

transact *v.* to do business, such as buying or selling, with another company

transparent *adj.* If rules, methods or business dealings are *transparent*, they are clear and people can see that they are fair and honest.

treasury *n.* a government department that controls the money that the country collects and spends

trust *n.* an arrangement by which someone has legal control over your money and usually invests it for you, or an organisation that does this

trustee *n.* someone who controls money or property that is in a trust for someone else

U

unfair competition *n.* an area of law relating to unacceptable practices that can give companies unfair trading advantages (US antitrust law)

unpredictable *adj.* If something is *unpredictable*, you cannot say in advance with certainty what is going to happen.

uphold *v.* If a court *upholds* a decision made by another court, it states that the decision was correct.

V

validity *n.* legal acceptability

verdict *n.* an official decision made in a court of law or other organisation that has authority

vest *v.* If shares, stocks, etc. are *vested*, they are owned by someone.

vested interests *n.pl.* a group of people with strong reasons for wanting something to happen because they will gain an advantage from it

veto *v.* to officially refuse to allow something to happen, especially something other people have agreed

vice versa in the opposite way, e.g. Person A tells Person B about their legal training, and *vice versa* (so Person B tells Person A).

virtually *adv.* almost; very nearly

W

wave through *v.* to allow without much delay or question, e.g. Security officials *waved* the car *through* the checkpoint, without stopping it.

welfare *n.* general comfort and security

withholding tax *n.* tax held back by financial institutions from payments to investors, and paid directly to the tax authorities

without prejudice to without affecting; without taking anything away from

witness *n.* someone in a court of law who tells the court what they saw or what they know about a crime

Useful websites

Legal resources

1. British and Irish Legal Information Institute (BAILII)
   www.bailii.org
   - Gives access to freely available public legal information.
   - Provides links to worldwide law resources, e.g. World Legal Information Institute (WLII), and legal institutes in Asia, Africa, Australia, Canada, Europe, New Zealand, the USA and other countries.
2. HG.org Legal Directories
   www.hg.org/lawfirms-assocint.html
   A comprehensive directory of law firms and lawyers' associations around the world, e.g. associations for lawyers for commerce, sports, the environment, human rights, entertainment, young lawyers, women lawyers, independent lawyers, judges, law teachers and law associations in many different countries.

Legal language

1. Plain English Legal Guide
   www.plainenglish.co.uk/free-guides.html
   An A–Z guide of legal phrases, written in jargon-free plain language
2. Clarity
   www.clarity-international.net
   An international association promoting the use of plain legal language. It encourages lawyers to use clear language and to avoid 'legalese' where possible.